What's a Parent to Do?

Ideas & Options for Parents of Bright Teens

**Edited by
Mark R. DeLong, Ph.D.
and
Webb C. Howell**

TAG Books
Durham, North Carolina

A TAG Books publication
Published by the Duke University Talent
Identification Program and Journalistic, Inc.

Duke University Talent Identification Program
1121 West Main Street
Suite 100
Durham, NC 27701

Journalistic, Inc.
4905 Pine Cone Drive
Suite 2
Durham, NC 27707

ISBN 0-9637364-7-7

Contents

Acknowledgments

No book is the work of a single person, but this book, perhaps more than some, is the handiwork of many talented individuals.

Thanks to David Goldstein, executive director of TIP, who allowed this project to happen and contributed especially to the chapter on "The Needs of Academically Talented Teenagers." Others at TIP who provided guidance include Joy Baldwin and Ramon Griffin.

Greg Sanders of Journalistic, Inc. played a key role in making assignments, editing manuscripts, and helping shape many chapters. He also authored the chapter on "What to Do About Getting Ahead," and prepared the chapter "What to Do About Getting Into College," along with Patricia O'Brien. Portions of that chapter were excerpted from "Why Great Students Don't Get In," by Debra Wingood, and "Avoiding the Blaze-Orange Sport Jacket," by Willoughby Johnson, both of which originally appeared in *The College Guide for Academically Talented Students*.

Others who contributed their time and writing talents to this book include Eric Larson, Lea Davis, Vernon Apperson, and Shannon Powers. We especially thank all those who were generous with their time in granting interviews, including David Hartman and Michael Yoo.

Those who have contributed to the design and production of this book include Rosie Haller, art director, and David McClure, cartoon illustrations. Finally, thanks to all staff of the Duke University Talent Identification Program and Journalistic, Inc., without whose efforts this book would not have been possible.

Preface

What's a Parent To Do? goes beyond the day–to–day problems parents face and seeks to describe opportunities for bright-
minded teenagers. Every book has its audience, and we hope ours
is evident. By setting our sights on academically talented teenagers,
we implicitly assume that bright children are different from average children. And because they are different, they present different
challenges to parents, who must respond appropriately.

The issues we address are generally positive: How to make
your child a better student; How to take a more meaningful trip;
How to help your teen find the right college. That's not to say that
parents of bright teenagers don't also face issues that raising any
teen presents. *What's a Parent To Do?* doesn't address those issues
because, we think, those concerns are more about being a teenager than about being bright. As you will see, however, being bright
doesn't necessarily mean your teen will make good decisions.

Your teen needs your help. Providing your teen guidance is
certainly more complicated than it was when he or she went to
elementary school. As a teen, your child wants to make his or
her own decisions—indeed should want to make them. You will
be sought more for advice, and if you give it constructively, your
teen will welcome—even be relieved with—the advice you give.
Parenting a bright teenager should be as rewarding as it is exciting, and we hope that *What's a Parent to Do?* will make that
reward more likely. In this book we inform three ways.

First, we have focused on parenting highly able teens, and we
have sought to present what makes parenting them distinctive and
challenging. We have looked upon parents' role more complex-
ly. Though we dedicated a good portion of the book to school

matters, we look at issues in education more broadly, recognizing that school is a part—and sometimes not even the most important part—of educational success for academically talented teenagers.

Second, we present basic information and issues that relate quite generally to parenting talented teens, in effect forming a toolbox of concepts and points to consider. Sometimes these might describe, say, trends in schooling or kinds of involvements in (and expectations for) schools. The information might help you discover a new way of doing something that you are used to doing anyway, like taking the family vacation. Sometimes, you will discover in the concepts a reason why what you have been doing all along happens to have been successful—and how you can apply that concept to other matters of parenting.

Third, we point you to other resources, because by the time you finish reading parts of this book, we hope that you will have a list of your own questions, the kind of questions that relate to your own parenting situation.

Organizationally, the book has three sections: The first describes in general some broad concepts and issues about the "average" teenager and about schooling. The second looks at particular practices of family life and helps you think about them strategically—always asking the question: "How does this help my child?" The third section describes the kinds of pressure talented teens feel and presents, in interview format, some talented former teens—ones who are beginning autonomous lives and are following courses of their own making.

What's a parent to do? Perhaps this book will lead you to some of the answers. We hope, too, that it encourages you to ask more questions. We live in a wonderful time, even with all its problems, when the human experience is discovering new opportunities. As you guide your teen into that world, we hope you can do so with insight and humor. A little grace helps, too.

The Editors
Durham, North Carolina
June 1993

What's a Parent to Do?

Preparing Students Today to be Scholars for a Lifetime

by Margaret Evans Gayle

More than one hundred years before today's students were born—in 1874 to be exact—a man wrote a book in which he described, in detail, a trip to the moon. He predicted accurately man's first trip to the moon, which became reality in 1969. He said in his book, *From the Earth to the Moon and Back*, that an American pilot would fly to the moon in an upright ship propelled by fuel, launched from the southeastern tip of the United States, and tracked by a telescope in the Midwest. The same man also wrote the blueprint for the first atomic submarine, television, satellites, hot air balloon travel, and many of our modern appliances. But he did it all in fiction, and his biography has been entitled *The*

Man Who Invented the Future. Today, we need scientists and creators like Jules Verne, people who can invent and solve complex problems for the future. Our children are our hope for the future. Our gifted and talented children are our hope for creating a quality future for the planet. We must find better ways to help them create their own visions and experiences for the future.

The changes and challenges of the future in which today's students will study, work, live, love, and enjoy will pose more complex problems than at any other time in modern history. We are living in a most exciting time, a time to invent; to explore new worlds; to use new technologies to solve many of the world's problems with learning, diseases, and the environment; to improve our status as human beings; and to be active in a world that is unfolding in a biotechnology and chemical era. And in these times—we have, also, the most challenges ever, regarding social, political, philosophical, economic, and technological changes.

The Big C's are important to the understanding of the world and in the preparation of citizens for the future: Change, Complexity, and Challenges; Choices and Chances; Community; Credibility and Competence; Competitiveness and Cooperation; Creativity and Courage; Commitment and Caring. All are necessary for us to create our visions for the future and to plan for them.

Changes and Challenges

We cannot predict the future, but we can analyze the trends and the "rampant changes" that have moved modern societies quickly through the information age into a high tech global connection. Many of the changes and challenges will require complex solutions by informed and well-educated citizens.

Many of our current students will work for global companies, which will require them to have a thorough understanding of world geography, languages, and cultures. Every occupation and profession will be impacted by the influences of the high tech revolution, from the building trades to medicine and law. All businesses are undergoing major restructuring: firing middle managers, making teams responsible for decisions, cutting fringe benefits, and paying lower wages. Out of the top Fortune 1000 companies at the beginning of the 1980s, only half are still in business in their present form. From boardrooms to classrooms, the struggle to understand these changes and to adapt to them will be awesome.

Many students born in this decade will live into the twenty-second century. Medical miracles designed to prolong life will create new legal problems for citizens who live out their lives in the twenty-first century. The completion of a DNA profile for human beings, within a few years, will usher in complex problems for citizens and the medical and legal professions. The end of the cold war, worldwide, requires a more global approach to understanding people from many cultures, religions, and economic perspectives. Today's students will live in the superhighway of information and technology. They will be "knowledge workers"; their jobs and their potential for the future will depend on how well they can use technology and analyze information for solving problems. The potential for today's students to own their own businesses or to work at home will be greater than ever before. All of these trends will require constant re-training and updating of knowledge and the utilization of emerging technologies.

Preparing students to understand the future and the trends that will shape what they want to be and do when they grow up is critical. The most important change in thinking about education is to teach students to be learners, not knowers. *The greatest mission for education, especially for those students who are gifted and talented, is to build their capacities for learning—which will require exposure to many experiences in critical thinking and problem solving.*

Building Capacities for Learning

All children are born to learn. All experiences become learning experiences, either positive or negative, and set the tone for their behaviors for a lifetime of learning. Play and "alone time" are important to building capacities for learning. Children need this time to experiment, with guidance from parents or others who are responsible for them. Gifted and talented students need experiences that challenge and motivate them to expand their horizons across many disciplines. Their creativity needs expression in areas of interest which many schools cannot provide. All experiences, curriculum, and resources should be the exercise equipment for the development of their minds. If these experiences, curriculum, and resources are poor in quality or are not accurate representations, then much damage is done to the learner. Nell Eurich, writing in Alvin Toffler's *Learning for Tomorrow*, believes that "if teachers do not understand the future, they will do tragic damage to those they teach."

Building capacities for learning requires new ways of evaluating learners and their schools. Many of the trends in education today show how hard we are struggling with reforming all aspects of the learning process, but with little dramatic change in the way we teach and test students. As a nation, our educational system ranks *at the bottom* of the top fifteen industrialized nations in the world, when our students are compared on the International Assessment of Educational Progress. Experiments in outcome – based education, cooperative learning, community service, and many other model programs will help students in developing more competencies and with learning to work in teams with diverse groups of people. These are important skills for living and working in a democratic society. But many of these experiments do not provide students with more up-to-date resources or individual assistance with specific learning questions and problems.

John Dewey, a noted educator whose career spanned from the 1880s to the 1950s, believed that children have many questions of their own and that they need them answered. He believed that students learned by doing, by being involved with real-life experiences. He believed that in a democratic society, "the mission of education is to teach students to be their own scientists" (*John Dewey and American Democracy*, by Robert B. Westbrook, 1991).

Dewey's research is popular again with new possibilities for raising the level of academic standards for all students and providing the academically talented with advanced levels, not just additional assignments within lower-level courses. As a role model for democracy in the '80s, America lagged behind as a role model in educational achievement. Our K-12 students are behind their counterparts in other major countries in mathematics and science. How can this happen in a country that has the best universities in the world? With the realization that America continues to decline in education, major efforts were undertaken during the '80s to improve education.

National Trends

Since 1983, when the alarming *Nation At Risk* report documented America's educational decline in the world, much effort and millions of new dollars were expended under "reform efforts." Many of these efforts improved student achievement but for the most part still left American students behind their peers worldwide. One of the most disturbing facts, as Marvin Cetron and I pointed out in *Educational Renaissance*, is that "our brightest twelfth-graders, the top five percent of those who have taken advanced math courses, when matched against their counterparts from eight other countries in standardized algebra and calculus tests, come in dead last."

What is wrong with America's schools after a decade of reform and what can we do to make them right?

Politicians, business leaders, and educators, alarmed by the continued decline in student scores, decided in 1989 that it was time for America to set national goals and world-class standards, with a focus on dramatically improving student achievement by the year 2000.

All other major industrialized countries have educational goals that produce their desired results. America's constitution gives every state the responsibility for educating students, but not every state is equal in the ability to deliver quality curriculum and resources and to pay for well-qualified teachers. National public opinion polls reflect that all citizens believe quality education is critical to America's future. It is with this belief that the President of the United States and the National Governors' Association formed alliances to set national goals and standards for all students with a national strategy targeted for the year 2000.

America 2000, a bi-partisan national strategy developed under the Bush Administration, was designed to move America's public education system to first in the world by the year 2000. President Bush and the National Governors' Association initiated a decade-long strategy to increase educational performance at all levels. With the election of Governor Bill Clinton as President in 1992, this strategy is now known as *Goals 2000*. The goals remain the same, but the legislation is known as: "Goals 2000: Educate America Act." The national goals, in brief, are:

1. all children ready to learn;

2. 90 percent graduation rate;

3. all children competent in core subjects; (English, mathematics, science, history, and geography)

4. first in the world in math and science;

5. every adult literate and able to compete in the work force; and

6. safe, disciplined, drug-free schools.

It remains to be seen whether a new Education Act and the additional layers of federal government committees can produce the necessary leaps that will be required by the states in order to meet the goals by the year 2000. In any event, the hope within all the national, state, and local activity is that expectations of American students will be raised.

Community and Parental Involvement

Critical to the success of the national and state efforts will be parental and community involvement. Many of the reform models or projects, especially with outcome–based education, have resulted in split communities, because of the lack of communication by school boards to parents and the community.

Gaston County, in the shadow of Charlotte, North Carolina, won a New American Schools multimillion dollar grant for dramatic changes, which included allowing children to learn at their own pace in year–round schools, doing away with grade levels, and requiring community service. "Odyssey," the winning proposal, created havoc in the communities, because parents were not included in the process and did not understand the changes when the program was announced. Recently, according to one official source, the grant was cancelled because the program was too "vague" and "theoretical," which was the original complaint of the parents. Much damage has indeed been done in the name of reform. Reform efforts without parental and community involvement will not work in today's diverse populations. Education professionals and board members have new responsibilities in the communication of reforms and keeping people informed of the changing trends.

It is imperative that parents become informed about the trends toward outcome based models, new curriculum frameworks and assessments, and the recent research in multiple intelligences and learning styles. It is the right and responsibility of all parents to be involved in the education of their children.

More parents are aware of the problems and what will be required for meeting the challenges of the future and their roles in building expectations for their children. But until parents, students, professional educators, and "grassroots citizens" value education for all and believe that all can learn at high levels, little will change for individual students. And we could arrive in the year 2000 still behind on the world scene. The key message is that someone has to be a champion for every child, to understand

and to be able to evaluate their specific needs and interests, and to motivate them to achieve at high levels so that their futures are not limited. We need champions—parents, teachers, volunteers—who will be there for children as models who value learning as a lifelong process.

The Home As The Center of Life and Learning Again

The home is becoming the center of life again as employers encourage parents to go home to work, either part-time or full time. This trend, coupled with the year-round school trend, will provide more opportunities for parents to make choices about the time that children can be with them and the time of year that they will be in school. The traditional school year is difficult to change because of the attitudes built over decades within the industrial model of work and school. The school calendar can be altered dramatically with the emerging interactive technologies available to the home and other institutions such as public libraries and museums. In the next few years, all homes will have the capability of receiving and interacting with educational resources that will be of entertainment quality. The difficult questions are:Who will have access? How will schools change as a result? What impact will these changes have on home life and work life? No one can predict the impact. Human factors will continue to determine home life as we move into the interactive world of multimedia, which at the present belongs to Nintendo and Sega.

Interactive Multimedia Technologies

With today's computer technology and the promise of tomorrow's interactive multimedia and virtual reality tools, we are closer to providing the best of all worlds for students, especially those students who can move ahead without a lot of repetition. Human teachers' roles will change to being coaches, facilitators, and mentors, and the interactive multimedia technologies will provide students with individual state-of-the-art resource tools and feedback to their problem-solving activities. Today, most of our schools, even expensive private schools, have obsolete reference and textbooks. Think of the changes in the world and consider that none of these changes get into textbooks for years. Teachers get little staff development in the updating of the subjects that they teach. Therefore, parents need to invest in technology that will provide their children with the latest resources and tools for improving their learning capacities.

Invest in Technology and Online Services

Investing in a computer for learning for the entire family is important. The computer is the basic tool for the future and is just as important as the pencil and tablet of past generations. The computer is a natural tool for teaching the writing process and for researching all subjects to make sure that the data is accurate. This process of outlining, writing, revising, spell-checking, and grammar-checking builds a critical thinking capacity for the student and provides one of the most important lifelong learning skills, with constant feedback to the learner. Writing is a process that improves dramatically once the mechanics are learned.

In addition to a computer, the next most important tool for building independence in student learning is a modem that can access a network of magazines, reference books, and other resources. Students can become part of a network of other students and teachers, not only in America but throughout the world. New consumer services that provide "video on demand" will be in homes within the next year or two. Students and parents will be able to tap into an entire film library without leaving home. These film libraries will include current events and history, as well as documentaries on a host of subjects.

New online services are getting cheaper for the consumer. These services are more user-friendly, with newly-designed special services such as *America Online* or *CompuServe*, which provide a network for teachers, parents, and students to discuss and to access the latest information, research studies, and resources from the National Education Association, the Association of Supervision of Curriculum and Development, CNN, Turner Educational Services, and the Smithsonian Institution. Access to *Internet*, *ERIC*, and a host of other databases make this a popular choice for students and their teachers. Parents can keep up with the latest trends in the research of the brain and learning practices.

Travel Into the Real World

Travel to museums, libraries, and historical and scientific places provides students with rich resources to evaluate their interests and to see their own potential in the future. From a very early age, children seem to love science and do math problems. What happens to shut down their natural curiosity as they grow older? There is much evidence that when students ask questions that are not answered, they quit asking. Over time, even smart students will quit asking the questions. Since schools have large classes, it is important that parents provide ways for students to discuss their experiences, to solve problems, and to experience as many real-life events as possible.

Since we do not know what all the jobs of the future will be, it is difficult for students to understand what they may want to be when they grow up. School counselors will become the most important professionals in the future, provided they get the training and the resources to stay current with job markets and college and technical programs. Today, most of the up-to-date databases are on-line services.

A major trend emerging to help students develop an awareness of jobs, a work ethic, and citizenship is community service. Community service is a current trend gaining national attention. The goal most often stated is the belief that students practice basic skills and learn citizenship from being involved in real job situations and with people who can be role models. Limited research shows that perhaps the most important reason for providing community service through schooling is to give students the experience of many areas of interest while they are taking their required courses. Some school districts are making community service a requirement for all students. Again, this trend needs to be evaluated carefully as more local school districts adopt it.

Another exciting trend is the development of more museums that not only have artifacts of the past but also focus on emerging technologies and issues, such as biotechnology, recycling, world cultures, and medicine. America is rich in marine and wildlife habitats, zoos, museums, historical sites, and public libraries. These museums will continue to be places to visit, but as our electronic superhighway is finished, many of these museums will be accessed through interactive multimedia units in the homes and other learning environments.

Traveling abroad is becoming cheaper with increased flights and special promotions. Understanding of other cultures and exposure to a variety of languages will be crucial to the students who want access to good jobs in the future. Growing up with diverse cultures, learning foreign languages, and traveling will provide students with the important skills of negotiation and getting along with people. Most of our gifted and talented students will have opportunities to work for global companies. They must not wait until college to begin to think about those possibilities.

Reading Across the Disciplines

There are few things that can take the place of reading a variety of books and journals. Being able to speed read and to read with understanding are critical to students. Colleges require numerous major readings. Getting required reading lists from colleges or public libraries, at the beginning of high school, can help students organize their reading habits and build a master set of notes for long term use. Many high school English teachers can provide additional reading lists.

In *Education of a Wandering Man,* the popular western writer Louis L'Amour, a high school dropout, kept a list of all the books that he read over a lifetime. He said he "knew what he didn't know," so he read all kinds of books when he had an interest in learning something. Students need encouragement and assistance to be able to find stimulating books and materials that focus on an interest at the time when they are interested. Many students find reading slow and boring. In those cases, taking a speed reading course and learning that one can read with understanding without having to read every word is crucial. Gifted and talented students find many books boring and often drop out or disengage from the reading process. When this happens, look for videos, magazines, computer programs, or other kinds of books that can provide the same information.

Students have a long life ahead of them. Gifted and talented students will have wonderful opportunities to invent, create, and to solve many of the problems that are facing us today. They should have time during their youth to explore many avenues of interests, keeping in mind that a balance of liberal and fine arts and the sciences, along with technology, will ensure unlimited opportunities for additional education, work, and leisure. We must hope that our most gifted and academically talented students will take the leadership to use their gifts and their "multiple intelligences" to help shape our future as a nation.

Martin Luther King came forward with the dream of being judged by the content of character, and his dream became the dream of his people and ultimately the dream of America. Jules Verne's visual fiction became our sophisticated technologies—our trips around the world and to the moon and beyond. Ann Sullivan's teaching touched Helen Keller and helped her communicate with the world and provided us with a superior model for potential within a handicapping condition. Susan Anthony's dream, vote, and arrest one hundred years ago made it possible for our daughters to vote today and ultimately to have a voice in democracy.

The Big C's may be more important to our future than the Big A's that we strive for in school. The future holds for each of us unlimited possibilities—both positive and negative. We can be passive players on the world stage, or we can work hard to use our talents to develop possibilities that we may prefer by taking responsibility for our own education and learning over a lifetime. Louis L'Amour said it best: "Only one who has learned much can fully appreciate his ignorance."

Today is our future; it is all we have. It is important to honor the past, but it is more important that we live in the present and for the future. I challenge parents to plan as if we will do just that.

Exceptionally Average

You'll find a lot of "average" characteristics in your son or daughter— despite above-average intellect.

Bill Harris, a resident of Minneapolis, is the father of an above-average 14-year-old. His son, Todd, has been enrolled in gifted classes since the third grade and now takes the toughest classes in junior high. But Bill is aware that his son's attitude toward his schoolwork may change.

"There's always a reverse peer pressure," Bill says. "It's not the pressure of 'Let's achieve,' but the pressure of 'Let's be average.'

"I think kids get mixed signals, and sometimes it can't be helped. In school, you want your child to be above average. Socially, you hope he will fit in, be normal. But you also hope that if everyone is at a party, drinking and cutting up, and they decide to go for a ride... Once again, you beg for your child to be different."

So what exactly do we want from our bright teenagers? We accelerate them in school, but on social matters we tell them to slow down. We do everything we can to get information to them, but when we try to warn our kids about something like LSD on the backs of postage stamps, they look at us like we're the biggest idiots in the world. And if we don't warn them... Well, there are thousands of parents in emergency rooms every year wondering how it happened to them. When we were growing up, about all we learned was not to talk to strangers. Today, teenagers need more.

Often, we as parents don't have a clue as to what our teenagers need to hear and what they don't. Certainly the issues are made even more difficult because—let's face it—things have changed a lot since we were kids. In order to help parents answer some of these questions, experts have developed the concept of the "average teenager," an imaginary figure which can sometimes help you understand the life and lifestyle of your own teen. That's not to say that your teen's likes, dislikes, plans, actions, or makeup are mirrored by these profiles. The average teenager does not exist in your home; these profiles only help in comparing your teen to others, in giving you a better point of reference.

What's more, the average teenager and the average academically talented teenager can be very different. So it is appropriate to look at both. But a word of caution: Don't confuse "average" and "normal"—or the average teen's behavior to appropriate behavior. Only you can set those guidelines.

Who are the post-boom teens?

Teenagers make up less of the population today than when you were growing up. Although there are 13.5 million teenagers in the US between the ages of fourteen and seventeen, they make up only 5.4 percent of the population in this country, down from 7.9 percent in 1975 when the largest group of baby-boomers started coming of age. Although the numbers of teens are expected to climb, many places, like college admissions offices, are feeling the teenage population drought. But fewer applicants still won't make it easier for the best students to get into the best schools. Generally, it's the smaller, less competitive schools that are hurting for applicants, although few schools will admit it.

For many teenagers, family life is much different than when you were growing up. Nearly one-fourth of kids under eighteen live in a single-parent household. That's not true, however, if you're gifted or among the very few highly gifted. In one study, ninety-two percent of the highly gifted teens and eighty-six percent of gifted teens come from two-parent homes. One less parent can mean one less paycheck. Today the median income for

"MOM! MOM! WHERE ARE MY SHOES?"

all families is $39,000. However, in a study by the Duke University
Talent Identification Program, the average yearly household
income in 1988 was $65,000 for the highly gifted and $45,000
for the talent search population as a whole. At least some of the
difference can be attributed to a two-income family. It's good to
remember, though, that there are many gifted children in lower-
income families.

Since so many teens have single parents, or both married
parents working, new responsibilities have fallen to them. One duty,
previously left to parents, is grocery shopping. It should be no surprise, then, that a lot of media today is directed toward teens. Marketers
of soap suds and orange juice know teens show up every day at
the market and often make the decision of which brand to buy.
Teens today are spending a lot of their own money, too. Teens aged
twelve to nineteen years have an average of $60 per week in dis-
posable income—some $22 billion annually. Even kids as young
as ages eight to twelve—nearly one-fourth of them—have a paying job such as babysitting, mowing grass, or delivering papers.
So while teens today aren't in the numbers they once were, they are
in the malls and the markets—and making their presence known.

How does the average teen pass the time?

In general, school (the going-to part) still takes up most of
an average teenager's day. When it comes to homework, though,
many teens simply aren't hitting the books. SAT scores are one
indication: The average SAT for college-bound seniors in 1989-
90 was 424 for verbal, 476 for math, as compared to 424 verbal and 466 math in 1979-80.

As the parent of an academically talented teen, you know
your child is capable of work well above those scores. Perhaps sheer
brain power is one reason, but down the road, how much effort
your teen puts into homework will play a key role in the grades
he or she gets. Yet only one-fourth of thirteen-year-olds spend two
or more hours on homework each day.

What is the average teenager doing instead of studying?

Thirty percent say they ride around in a car for fun on a daily basis. One-third play a musical instrument or sing every day, while one in ten does arts and crafts or creative writing.

The big drain on time is TV. Teens aged thirteen to seventeen watch a lot of TV, but teens at the younger end of the age range watch the most. It should be no surprise that teens with better grades watch less TV and spend more time reading. But the real question for parents is whether all the TV viewing is cause for concern. Statistically, teens watch television less often than their parents. Yet television is such a large part of the lives of those who grew up with it—which now includes many parents—that simply turning it off for good may not be a solution in most families. It may also be an unnecessary one.

One high school guidance counselor says, "Television is something teenagers use but don't rely on. Rather, they tend to follow the lead of other family members. If the family is active, the child will be active. Television often serves to fill a gap. The best way to squeeze out television is to fill that gap with something else."

Of all distractions in the house, the one that truly captures the average teenager's time and attention is the telephone, especially younger teens who don't have the benefit of a driver's license. In spite of the TV and telephone, teens are spending some time with computers and books. Above-average teens reported spending two hours a day reading, while their average counterparts spent about twenty minutes less. And the technology explosion has seen a meteoric rise in the use of home computers. One *Boy's Life* study reported that three-fourths of their readers used a personal computer at home. For what? Games, games, and more games. Some 92 percent use their PC for entertainment. But there is hope. Seventy-five percent also used their PC for some kind of schoolwork. No report on the grades they received.

What's on the average teen's mind?

Although our teens may seem like they don't contemplate life, much less the dirty clothes basket, many are giving important thought to the kind of lifestyle they would like to be living.

One of the important questions they pose to themselves is, "How should I live?" Despite their ongoing effort to be independent, more often than not the teen's likely answer is, "Like my parents." In 1990, 70 percent of high school seniors agreed with their parents on such crucial topics as: "value of an education," "what to do with my life," and "religion." Roughly 40 percent agreed with their parents on: "how to spend money," "what is permitted on a date," or political views.

Irma Zandl, teen prognostication guru for major corporations, notes that teens are shying away from fast-lane lives. Themes for the future include: owning a business or free-lancing, hiking and camping, going to church, larger families, and country music. The fact that teenagers, who are traditionally viewed as being at war with their parents, tend to think like their parents is not the paradox it may seem. Teens tend to agree with parents on large issues but disagree on small ones, if for no other reason than to test the limits set for them.

Rather than particular concerns, perhaps the most important concern for parents is their teen's overall happiness. A survey of Minnesota students found that one-fourth of them had felt sad, discouraged, hopeless, stressed-out, or unhappy with their personal lives. Another survey of eighth to tenth graders found that one-third of the female students and 15 percent of the male students had felt sad and hopeless during the previous month. While many, if not most, of these feelings can be attributed to the universal problems of growing up, some may be signs of deeper problems, and parents need to stay in-tune with their teens on these matters. Doing great in school and being happy are different, and the wise parent doesn't assume they go hand-in-hand.

How active is the average teen?

About half of teenagers do physical exercise, with the most popular methods being swimming and bicycling. In a survey which asked teens what sports activities they had participated in at least six times the past year, 55 percent swam, 45 percent cycled, one-third played basketball, and one-fourth went camping or played volleyball.

One of the main reasons for exercising among teens is a very adult one: to lose weight. *Forecast* magazine's fifth annual "Teen and Food Nutrition Study" in 1990 showed that 43 percent of the teenagers had tried to lose weight in the past year. Cutting desserts and sweets was the most popular way to do it. Exercising more and skipping meals were second and third, respectively. It's no wonder that only one in ten teens ranked fruit as their favorite snack, with most still preferring potato or corn chips, cookies, candy, and ice cream.

When the weekend rolls around, movies or socializing in the local mall is popular. Teenagers are also the most sought-after victim for rape, robbery, and assault—and malls are often targets for would-be perpetrators.

Like it or not, the average teenager is having sex (and every teen is capable). Each year, about a million teenagers become pregnant (11 percent of teens from fifteen to nineteen years of age), giving the United States the highest rate of any industrialized country. Half of them have abortions while the other half give birth, most out of wedlock. While numbers of teenage pregnancy declined significantly between 1972 and 1985, new numbers may show an increase. In 1979, a little more than half of all seventeen year olds said they were sexually active; in 1988, that number jumped to almost three-fourths.

Fortunately, in response to fear of both AIDS and pregnancy, condom use among teenage boys has more than doubled: from 21 percent to 58 percent. And teens know the risks: Eighty-two percent said it is not inconceivable that they could get AIDS, and more than three-fourths disagreed with the statement that "using condoms to prevent AIDS is more trouble than it's worth."

On the dreaded subject of drugs, if one counts alcohol and nicotine in the lot, then chances are the average teenager has used drugs. In 1989, 91 percent of teens drank alcohol at least once, while 66 percent smoked tobacco at least once. Marijuana is still the most popular illegal drug, though its occasional use went down from 60 percent in 1979 to 44 percent in 1989.

To be average, or not to be average?

Of course, the litany of statistics on teens and teen behavior goes on and on. And you may be thankful that you don't have to raise the average teenager.

What is important is to understand that your bright teenager may well be average in many respects—not all of which are bad. Parents have the responsibility to consider the possibility that their teens are "average" in some ways and that their lives are impacted by these and other statistics. Parents need to be prepared to help their teens through the challenging teenage years.

The Needs of Academically Talented Teenagers

If you understand academic talent in a context beyond your home, you can help your teen reach full potential.

This chapter is the text of an interview with David Goldstein, executive director of the Duke University Talent Identification Program.

Beyond what every human needs, academically talented teens need one thing: to be intellectually challenged. Without that, their greatest gifts lie dormant, perhaps for a lifetime.

As a parent of a bright teenager, you probably aren't surprised at your child's ability. No doubt you remember countless nights of reading books to your child, or days in the backyard helping your child understand the wonders of a leaf. Yet when you have successfully guided your child into middle school, and now that child demonstrates high abilities in academics, you as a parent have done something right. But from middle school onward, teens have the ability to learn so much more, to challenge their intellect in ways they never dreamed. Your role is to make it all possible.

Where are schools in addressing the needs of academically talented students?

Gifted education in the United States has gone through a series of cycles. There was really nothing like gifted education as we know it until about the 1920s. But in the 1950s, there was a lot of attention paid to talented students after the Soviets put Sputnik into space. Then gifted education declined somewhat, but again in the 1970s, schools tried to pay more attention to the needs of talented students. It was in that climate that programs like the Duke University Talent Identification Program (TIP) began. Since the late 1970s, the state of public education in the United States for gifted and talented students has been on the decline, in part because of limited resources and in part because of a move toward mainstreaming, which provides comparable opportunities to all students regardless of their exceptionality. To some extent, mainstreaming is justified for students who are learning disabled because it gives those students more opportunities. But applying the same principals to gifted and talented students in fact reduces their opportunities.

It is difficult to come up with one all-encompassing characterization of gifted education, because it varies enormously from state to state. But the key to all of this is not so much whether states spend more or less money or provide greater or fewer hours in special classes. The whole idea of education is that children differ enormously from each other and educators have to be sensitive to that diversity and responsive to those needs. Students need different types of challenges and learning opportunities. For some students, one afternoon a week in a pull-out gifted program might be just the motivation and recognition that child needs. But there are many other children for whom that level of learning is simply a drop in the bucket and is essentially worthless. Those children need a very different type of experience, and it is that lack of flexibility in schools that is most troublesome.

Certainly in a perfect world where resources were no problem, circumstances would be better for gifted education. But there are some people who are simply opposed to singling out students as academically talented and providing those kids with services and programs that others don't have. The real goal of education in the United States should not be equality of outcome but equality of opportunity. All children have the right to develop their talents to the best of their ability. While some would argue that all kids should have the same outcome in education and that the kids who go very fast should be held back, no one would ever dream of applying the same standards to adults in the occupational domain. No less an icon than Thomas Jefferson wrote at great length about the idea that people are different in terms of their talents and that those talents should be allowed to develop. That some people are more talented than others—well, so be it. This is something we should celebrate rather than squash.

What about elitism?

So many people perceive that gifted education today is primarily for economically advantaged children, and these attitudes contribute to their sense that gifted education is elitist. But such charges that gifted programs are elitist are really false issues. Many schools have special programs for talented students, and they devote a great deal of resources to those programs even when resources are scarce. They have special teachers and equipment, and the programs are given a great deal of attention both in the school and in the local community. The students' achievements are celebrated, recognized, and honored. They are highly selective—only a very few kids qualify for these programs. Sound great? Well, of course, nobody has a problem with these programs because they are sports programs. Football, for example, is a program for gifted athletes that takes resources, special teachers, and special equipment. Yet when the domain is academics, some people get very squeamish.

Are we falling behind?

Our best and brightest students may no longer be as good as the best and brightest of other countries. However, we make the greatest attempt possible to educate all of our kids in the same kinds of classes. In other countries, kids are much more easily excluded from mainstream classes. So, to some extent, classes in the United States have a wider range of basic ability than classes in Germany or Japan or Taiwan—and so, we are comparing all American kids to a selected sample of kids in other countries.

If we do less well in educating our average child, it is in part because we expect more of our schools than other countries do. Our schools have become not just places to teach our children reading, writing, and arithmetic, but also places to teach children about sexuality, alternative lifestyles, and on and on and on. Schools have become social laboratories, vehicles for fighting political battles that should be fought elsewhere. We put more and more burden on our teachers, and all of these things take time away from learning skills. In other countries, schools are much more narrowly focused.

There is some good research, coming out of Harold Stevenson's lab at the University of Michigan in particular, that finds a much stronger commitment to education in families in the Far East than in the United States. We as a society don't value learning and education as much as other cultures do, but there is a success story in this country that no one ever talks about: higher education. The American university system is still the envy of the world. We, a country of roughly 250 million people, have over three thousand institutions of higher learning. Japan has half our population and only about four hundred institutions of higher learning. The diversity of American higher education is incredible. A student can find a rich variety: big, small, private, public, religious, non-denominational, single sex, co-ed, technical, et cetera, et cetera, et cetera. The world's elites still come to the United States for higher education. Students in China are desperate to come to the United States to study. If you look at rankings of world class universities, most of them are American schools, and that is something we should be enormously proud of.

What role do programs like TIP play in all this?

TIP works outside public education, and to some extent that is a strength because we don't siphon off resources from other types of public programs—we aren't competing in the arena for a limited pool of taxpayer dollars. Even if public schools were everything we dreamed they could be, there would still be a need for programs like TIP, because even the most progressive schools can't fully meet the needs of all their students. Kids are different from one another, and a very academically talented youngster still needs the kind of challenge and peer group experience that only a program like this can provide.

We hear a lot of talk in Washington about world class standards, and, more than any other place in the United States, TIP is showing what those world class standards should be. To use a sports analogy: Forty years ago, no runner had ever run a mile in under four minutes, and it was thought to be impossible. But once someone broke that barrier—and it now seems almost routine—it raised the expectations for all athletes. When a seventh-grader shows he or she can get a 1440 out of 1600 on the SAT—like one student in our talent search just did—it raises expectations about what youngsters are capable of. All students benefit from higher expectations.

We have grossly underestimated what kids can learn under the right circumstances, and TIP has shown that kids can not only learn tremendous amounts—certainly much more than the kids themselves ever imagined—but can have the time of their lives doing it. We show kids that school can be more fun than anything else they have ever done.

What should parents know about nurturing academic talent?

Parents frequently express their frustration at the lack of guidance as to what they should do to nurture the talents of their children. Often, what is best for their kids—two parent households or greater financial resources—isn't possible. Teens who are identified as academically talented tend to come from families that are above average in terms of income and parental education. They are more likely to come from two-parent homes. Still, raising an academically talented child depends on a large number of factors, most of which have to be functioning in your favor. Research suggests that children who are talented can overcome the loss of a parent in the home or the lack of a quality primary or secondary education, or some other factor. But if two or three or four major factors are working against the child, then it is unlikely that the child's talent will be developed.

Income is a relevant issue insomuch as income is often correlated with ethnicity. Asian-Americans are over-represented in talent searches for academic ability because their parents have more education—largely due to selective immigration. African-Americans are often under-represented. Still, it is not money *per se*, but the ability to provide opportunities with that money, that affects academic talent. Single parents, with one–income households, are also under-represented in talent search populations. Even with the fee waivers and tremendous amount of scholarship money provided for summer programs, we know that many impoverished families are discouraged from trying. Very often there is what psychologists call "learned helplessness" that is sometimes associated with poverty. People have been worn down to the point where they simply stop trying.

Even more subtle disadvantages of income, like where there aren't books in the house or where the student may come from a rural environment lacking in opportunities, affect the development of academic talent. Those kinds of factors have to be taken into account. Academic talent is found everywhere, though, and there is absolutely no evidence of any scientific merit to suggest that one ethnic group is more capable than another, economic factors notwithstanding.

What academically talented teenagers need most of all is a good deal of encouragement and support from the family. That is absolutely key. School experiences should, at least in some respects, be challenging—not that every teacher has to be stimulating, but there should be at least one teacher to inspire your teen. Taking advantage of summer opportunities is very important because they give students opportunities they can't get in school.

The opportunity to explore a wide range of ideas and career possibilities is also important. People often believe that academically talented students are good in just one area, but it is important for you, as a parent, to be sensitive to the range of your child's talents. Give your child a chance to take a risk, even if the risk means not doing particularly well. Many academically talented kids become afraid of failure and become perfectionists. Many of these kids have done so well throughout their lives that the idea of taking a particular subject and not getting an A is terribly intimidating.

Is standardized testing so important?

Parents who seek to judge the talents of their children often turn to standardized tests. We do know that the younger the child, the less predictive the test. Infant IQ tests, for example, don't tell us very much at all. But by the seventh grade, standardized tests can provide an important piece of information. There is one critical thing to keep in mind. Research suggests that when youngsters do exceptionally well on these standardized tests, those scores are meaningful. But, if a child does not get a particularly high score on these tests, that does not mean the child has no talent. Standardized tests are somewhat like a thermometer—a very crude instrument. If a person has a temperature of 99°F, that may or may not indicate an illness. On the other hand, if that person has a temperature of 106°F, that is a meaningful number. If a twelve-year-old gets a 1400 on the SAT, that's a real number. But if that twelve-year-old gets an average score on the SAT, that's not particularly meaningful.

Those teens who do well on standardized tests generally continue to do well. These are not simply precocious kids who then slow down to the point where other kids have caught up with them. The very best students in the seventh grade ten years ago are now the very best students in the very best American colleges. When you discover your child is academically talented, be an advocate for the best possible education in your child's school. Be very alert to summer possibilities. Fill your house with as many books as you possibly can. Give your child as many opportunities as possible to explore and exercise his or her curiosity.

How do kids learn?

A definitive answer to that question is a long way off. We do know, however, that children learn at different rates and that learning takes time and effort. However, educational theories often enjoy periods of great popularity but then fade away, so parents need to have a certain amount of skepticism when evaluating so-called "revolutionary" ideas in education.

But there is no question that children have individual needs. Students should be allowed to learn at their own pace. So while they all may be learning the same subject, and they are all sitting in the same class, they don't all have to be on the same page on the same day. This concept of pacing is very important and, again, students have to be allowed to pursue their own interests and to go at their own pace.

Here's a good example: One third-grader complained that she had mastered the third grade math curriculum and was eager to move on, but the teacher couldn't allow her. She couldn't study fourth grade math until she got to the fourth grade. Parents must recognize this as a terrible thing to do to a child who is eager to learn—to say "No, you've learned all that you are supposed to learn and you can't learn any more this year."

If your child seems to express an interest in a particular topic, make an effort to see that he or she has an opportunity to explore that interest. Take him or her to the library, take a field trip on your vacation, swing by some place that speaks to whatever interests your child has. It is important for your child to know that you value and take his or her interests seriously. To a large extent, the things that make for a successful, innovative person in the corporate realm are not all that different than the things that make for an innovative, successful child. One has to be open to new ideas, be able to see subtleties that may elude other people.

So how are kids motivated to learn?

Many people look at motivation as some extra ingredient you have to add to an activity, but motivation is part and parcel to being in the right environment. When kids are given an emotionally supportive environment, are treated with respect, and are taken seriously, and when their intelligence is tested and their talents are challenged, motivation takes care of itself. Parents sometimes ask how TIP motivates our kids. We don't do *anything* to motivate the kids. They are already motivated—if they aren't motivated, that is a sign that something is wrong, that they are in the wrong setting. Motivation is, in a sense, "built in." People are inherently curious: Babies, for example, are constantly exploring, and kids are learning machines. Education, unfortunately, sometimes damages the machinery.

There are a number of people who are critical of programs for academically talented youngsters. These critics argue that doing well in school doesn't tell you much about doing well in life. While doing well in school is not a perfect predictor of doing well in life, it is at least a modest predictor. The real point is that there is no better predictor out there—because there is nothing that will predict who will do well in life. The fact that these programs don't do a better job of predicting who will do well in life isn't really a criticism of the programs.

There is no question that, to some extent, success in life

depends on ability, but success also depends on hard work. We have many myths about the nature of genius in our culture, but serious scholars who have looked at those individuals who were called geniuses tend to agree that they all worked very hard—that truly creative products don't spring fully-formed from their heads overnight—even though there are many stories that have sometimes been propagated by the creative people themselves.

We have a real love-hate relationship with genius in our culture. People love to tell stories, almost always untrue, about geniuses who were failures as children. There are stories about how Einstein couldn't add up a grocery list. Those are just patent nonsense. Einstein was always a good student and a talented person, and he worked hard. He liked to cultivate a somewhat offbeat image, but he was a consistently bright and hardworking person. The point is that hard work and talent go together, but we are better at predicting talent than we are at predicting motivation. There is no question that there are many people out there who, as adults, could make greater contributions to society but don't for a variety of reasons.

What good is gifted education?

Gifted education can instill the attitude that "Hard work can be fun." Kids who are gifted have all heard *ad nauseam* that hard work is necessary for success. They are constantly being exhorted to develop their talents, and they are being told over and over that they are the hope of the future. What children should learn for themselves is the joy of hard work, and that's what they should carry with them. The real tragedy of failing to recognize and nurture talent at an early age is that kids lose interest in school. There are so many kids who are mathematically talented who are totally turned off to math because their idea of math is just endless, boring worksheets going over the same exercises again and again. As children, they can't separate the drudgery of a poorly managed classroom from the subject matter.

Most big city school districts report that a hefty percentage of dropouts are kids who qualify for gifted programs but who are bored and turned off to school. And, of course, they then use their gifts and talents in socially unproductive ways. Instead of becoming the valedictorian of the class, they become the head of a gang.

People comment that Picasso or Edison didn't need gifted programs. Those kinds of comments reflect a real lack of sensitivity to what the issues are. There is no question that some people are going to achieve great things without the kinds of programs that TIP represents. But the more important question is: How many Edisons were never found because their talent was never nurtured? Some people will achieve great things even in the face of incredible adversity, but most people won't. Most people will be crushed by a lack of opportunity.

Student learning is a very complicated subject, and we are probably at least a century away from knowing how intelligence grows and develops. Virtually all human behavior is a complex interweaving of heredity and environment. Someone once used the analogy of Siamese twins who share the same nervous system and brain. In principle, it might be possible to separate them, but the technology to do that is decades away. The intellectual question of whether you can separate heredity and environment is comparable. The consensus in the field is that at least half of all intellectual development is attributable to environmental factors.

That is to say neither that heredity is unimportant nor that all children raised in a comparable way with dedicated teachers and loving parents and wonderful opportunities will become comparably talented. They won't. Some people are always going to be more outstanding than others.

What to Do About School

Your bright teen has options, especially if you make yourself heard.

Patricia Dade remembers her son Bobby's elementary school debut: "On the third day of school, I got a call from his teacher saying that Bobby wouldn't participate in reading group with the other boys and girls. Apparently he had told her, straight off, that the Dick-and-Jane-style primers were too boring, and he wouldn't waste his time reading them." Patricia explained to the teacher that her son had taught himself to read at age four and had been reading avidly ever since, but "that meant nothing to her. How could she expect him to be interested in 'see Spot run' when he was halfway through the Hardy Boys series?" After several weeks of haggling, Bobby finally was allowed to go to a second grade class for reading period.

But that was "just the beginning of our troubles with Bobby and school. He knew, and we knew, that he needed to work faster than the other kids his age, but school administrators dragged their heels about making any exceptions for him. As the years went on, kids started to resent him for doing so well, but, at the same time, he wasn't getting enough challenging work or moving fast enough to feel, I guess, fulfilled."

By his eighth-grade year, the situation was bad enough that Patricia and her husband began to look into other options. "I found out all I could, and I realized that my son wasn't going to get what he needed in that school." In the end, they decided to enroll Bobby in a private school where students could work according to their ability, not their age. There, he had challenging English classes and was allowed to skip third-year French. "I don't mean to imply that private school has to be the solution in every case like this. The costs for tuition and gas money were really high, but for Bobby it made all the difference," she says. "When he started at the new school, he told us he felt like he'd been let out of some kind of prison."

Bobby experienced the intellectual confinement and social fallout of what's called a lock-step curriculum. During the first part of this century, educators self-consciously began to envision schools modelled after assembly-line factories. After all, if the Ford company could use a fixed series of steps, done the same way and in the same order every time, to churn out car after perfect car, couldn't that amazingly successful method work in schools? Put children through a fixed progression of age-determined grade levels, turn the same academic crank at the appropriate times, and—*ka-chink*!—you'll churn out one perfect Model T student after another.

If you want to ensure that your gifted teen has the opportunity to learn as much and as quickly as she wants and needs to, you've most likely got some learning of your own to do. Jan Leppien, a researcher with the Teaching the Talented Program at the University of Connecticut, advises, "What parents need to do for their gifted children is to make sure they know how to ask the appropriate questions: How are my teen's special abilities and interests being met in the classroom? If my teen has already mastered the skills being taught, how can she avoid unnecessary review?"

What about ability grouping and cooperative learning?

You ask, "My son's school claims to use ability grouping as a way of serving students' special educational needs. He's highly gifted—will ability grouping be enough for him?"

Here's a decisive answer for you: Maybe, but maybe not.

Ability grouping, or the grouping of students for instruction according to their general ability or testing results, has been in use in American schools for more than seventy years. It takes many forms, some of which can benefit very able learners and others of which have not been successful.

There are two primary ways in which kids are grouped for learning. The first type always considers the child's ability to learn. Highly able learners are placed together and learn at an advanced pace, while students who need more time to learn are challenged at a slower pace. Schools call this homogeneous grouping, and a good case for it can be made with highly able students.

The second type of grouping, which school officials call heterogeneous grouping, is sometimes not really grouping at all. Parents are familiar with heterogeneous grouping, since it is pretty much the norm in schools that place students together by age groups—the typical class has a wide range of abilities, though that class will be composed of kids of roughly the same age. There is no regard for ability, whether that ability is in specific subjects or all subjects. However, many schools intentionally mix students of differing abilities in classrooms, following research indicating that such a mix of abilities will help most students achieve better.

Heterogeneous grouping can benefit gifted students, for instance when the student is less skilled in a particular area, Leppien says. Still, parents should worry if schools discourage, by policy, grouping any students by their abilities.

Schools across the country are enthusiastically adopting a relatively new form of heterogeneous instruction called cooperative learning. Rooted in socio-psychological theory that focuses on the benefits of cooperation over competition, cooperative learning uses groups of four to six learners who work together on a common academic task or project and, at the same time, cultivate social interaction skills and group interdependence. Picture this cooperative learning scenario: In a tenth-grade class studying the American Civil War, the teacher would give one student from each team materials on the Lincoln administration; their three teammates would receive information on Civil War battles, the impact of war on family life and social structure, and the history of slavery, respectively. All the students assigned to each area would then get together in "expert groups" to discuss and research their topic and decide how to present the information to their other team members. Back in their original groups, each member would explain what he learned in his expert group and would take notes on his teammates' presentations. Finally, the entire class would take a test on the Civil War, and each student would receive both an individual and a group grade.

Cooperative learning does come in many forms, some more effective than others for high-ability learners. Teachers should occasionally group gifted students together or allow them to choose their own groups, and should use cooperative learning for only a small proportion of classroom time. Some gifted educators cautiously approve a method called Group Investigation, which requires each group to decide what they will study and design their own curriculum. *However, even some of its most committed supporters concede that cooperative learning generally does not benefit the top five percent of learners.*

As a result, many advocates of gifted education are crying foul because school systems tend to overgeneralize the benefits of cooperative learning—which is relatively inexpensive and easy to implement—and see it as a panacea for schools' academic ailments.

As a result, funding that should have gone to financially-strapped gifted programs is often redirected toward cooperative learning programs, especially in middle schools.

Worse, many researchers charge, cooperative learning exploits gifted children by making them shoulder the burden of most of the group's work. "Cooperative learning, done correctly, can be good for moderately gifted through moderately slow learners," says Betty Maxwell, associate director of the Gifted Child Development Center in Denver, Colorado. But if the gap between the gifted student and her peers becomes too wide, "no learning will take place, plus frustration and resentment will result. Gifted students should not be forced to play the role of a peer tutor!" One gifted eighth grader even circulated a petition against cooperative learning, saying, "I don't think it's the student's job to make other students learn or want to learn. That's the teacher's job."

So how can ability grouping benefit my gifted teen?

The majority of researchers agree that gifted teens should associate and learn along with other teens of similar academic ability and drive—in other words, they benefit from at least some degree of ability grouping. "Gifted children desperately need a safe climate for sharing," says Maxwell. "Socialization, such as what is supposed to go on during cooperative learning, is not a need of gifted children—it is at the expense of the self-esteem that comes with learning and sharing with other kids on the same mental level. Gifted students need homogeneous peer groups."

Just how badly do they need them? The results are overwhelmingly positive in favor of ability grouping for high-ability learners. Research shows that when they're grouped with other kids according to ability and interests, gifted students jump at the opportunity to do abstract thinking and to tackle complex concepts. Overachievers proliferate and underachievers all but disappear. Positive self-concepts and senses of well-being flourish. Most of all, those gifted students escape from the boredom and frustration of constantly being limited, academically as well as socially, to a lowest common denominator. To deny the need for ability grouping, researchers say, is to deny the special instructional needs of gifted learners.

But a couple of caveats are in order.

First, don't accept charges that homogeneous grouping is elitist. You wouldn't expect a kid who can't read music to be in the marching band, or one who can't catch a football to make the varsity team. Grouping students according to their intellectual ability for certain purposes is much like grouping kids according to athletic ability for certain purposes. Besides, grouping gifted learners together actually encourages democratic values among them, argues Linda Silverman, director of the Gifted Child Development Center. "If you really want to create an elitist child, make her the smartest kid in the class for twelve years," she says.

Second, remember that ability grouping is not synonymous with "tracking," which implies restriction to a certain level of curriculum with no opportunity to move between levels.

"Tracking is a wholly different issue from ability grouping, and I think that the two have been blurred in popular interpretations of the literature," says Leppien. "We've got classroom teachers out there who don't know what they should and shouldn't be doing as far as grouping." Real, effective grouping practices are flexible—they provide a wide range of materials to all students, they are based on students' abilities and interests, and, importantly, they contain internal mechanisms that allow students to earn advancement to a higher level.

Where does ability grouping lead?

"My daughter has been in the highest ability group in both math and English since the fourth grade. She's now in ninth grade but she's still using the same textbooks as the rest of the students. Is this right?"

No, it's not.

By the time they reach the secondary school level, very able learners should be moving far beyond the basic skills and into more complex and abstract curricula. They need differentiated instruction and advanced learning materials that surpass the curricula reserved for their age-determined grade levels. If your daughter is held back to the pace of the more average learners in her class, she simply is not working to her full potential. What's more, many researchers in gifted education believe that a school's willingness to ability group and accelerate its brightest students is the litmus test of its commitment to meeting the needs of the gifted. If her school were truly amenable to serving your daughter's needs, she would certainly be ahead of the more average learners.

This question brings out an important point: Ability grouping, by itself, does not in any way lead to achievement among gifted students. Rather, grouping sets the stage for curriculum acceleration and advanced instruction, which do produce significant academic gains for the gifted. Acceleration doesn't just mean moving faster; it means molding the curriculum to fit an individual student's growing cognitive readiness and needs, letting quick learners move ahead at their own pace. It can be used in any school, costs next to nothing, and actually can save parents and schools money in the long run since many accelerated students complete high school and college in less time than usual.

Like any other issue, though, academic acceleration has its supporters and opponents. Studies and assessments of accelerated students continually show significant positive effects on their cognitive development and no negative effects on their social or emotional development. Accelerated students generally earn more academic honors and attend more prestigious colleges. In addition, they claim to have higher levels of self-esteem and motivation and to experience less boredom, frustration, and dissatisfaction in school. On the other hand, some educators and parents worry about making a child grow up too quickly just because he happens to be intelligent. There's even a name for it—the "hurried child syndrome"—and the symptoms include any acceleration practices that push gifted children through the curriculum without regard for their social or emotional development. Practiced correctly, though, acceleration constantly adjusts to the current needs of the individual child, taking into account his social and emotional needs as well as his academic needs.

So how do you know if you're being overbearing instead of helping your teen be all he or she can be? Usually your teen will tell you, though probably not in words. Sometimes the best of students would prefer not to disappoint Mom and Dad and will even go so far as adopting some self-destructive behaviors in order to send a message or provide an excuse for not meeting unreasonably high parental expectations.

If your teen withdraws, becomes chronically sullen and isolated, or fails to take an interest in something that's always been interesting before, you should probably try to find the trouble. Beyond that, scrutinize your expectations of your teen. Carefully ask yourself what pressures you have placed on your teen and why you have done so. Do you want to provide your teen with the means of developing his or her talents to the fullest? If so, consider what those talents are. The worst pressures you place on your teen assume strengths your teen doesn't have or agendas that are more your own rather than appropriate to your role as parents.

What forms does acceleration take?

Options for students (and parents) who want to accelerate might be somewhat limited, depending on the availability of resources and top-quality instructors in your teen's school. Generally speaking, though, acceleration techniques should be rather easy to implement in just about any school.

Schools might arrange a **special class structure** exclusively for gifted students—in other words, ability group the brightest students and give them a class of their own, either for a few subjects or for the entire curriculum. "Gifted children have always been somewhat vulnerable in the traditional classroom—they might give answers that are more complex than what the teacher wants or than their classmates can understand," says Betty Maxwell. "We've found that gifted children, girls in particular, do

"I THINK HE'S BEEN ACCELERATED"

a lot of self-censoring and closing down in the regular classroom." Given their own stomping grounds, free from negative peer pressure, very able learners can enjoy continuous progress through a flexibly-paced curriculum, encouraged by the progress of their gifted peers.

Acceleration comes in many forms with names like "telescoping" and "curriculum compacting," which are very similar in the ways that they appear in a course of study. Acceleration works especially well in junior high and high schools, because there is a more diverse course offering. It is possible for students to accelerate in specific subject areas or across the board. Students who excel in math, for example, can proceed through algebra I and II, geometry, trigonometry, and calculus—even skipping some of those—without regard to what grade they happen to be in. Acceleration in the high school years often means no more than tailoring study from courses already offered in the school to a pace that matches the student's ability.

If your teen demonstrates a high capacity, level of readiness, and motivation in an area or two, acceleration becomes a matter of enlisting an open-minded school guidance counselor, who will help him cut down on unnecessary study hall-type classes and work out a more condensed schedule. Gifted students who feel they have already mastered a full semester's or year's worth of knowledge in a subject area might want to try to arrange **credit by examination**, through which they can "test out" of a course and, if they score above an agreed-upon level, be awarded academic credit for the class. Each of these methods might very well put the accelerated student far ahead enough in the required curriculum to consider **early admission to high school or college**.

Acceleration can thrive in independent study. In the book *On Being Gifted*, which was written entirely by gifted students, one girl writes about the benefits of her independent study: "I thought I would feel lonely in a class all by myself, but instead I discovered some fantastic advantages. Not only do I have complete control over what I study, but also I have complete responsibility—there's no way I can hide behind other students and not prepare my reading. By myself in a class like this I can go completely at my own pace and do just what I want to, which is enormously stimulating." Gifted children report a preference for individualized work, and for those who have the intense curiosity and motivation to do coursework on their own, and who can find an ally in a teacher or knowledgeable administrator, independent study might be the ideal route for acceleration.

Grade skipping is perhaps the most traditional method of acceleration—it was popular in American schools until the 1920s, went out of style for a few decades, and is currently making quite a comeback. "Grade skipping is one very effective and inexpensive way to meet the needs of a very intellectually advanced student," says Maxwell; in fact, it can save one or two years' worth of school funding or tuition, as the case may be. During the 1950s and 1960s, grade skipping earned a bad reputation from psychologists who feared for students' emotional and social development. Those fears have been almost completely disproved, says Maxwell. "Researchers are finding, and have been finding for some time, that skipping a grade or grades does work and does not damage the student, socially or otherwise," she says.

But use common sense. These days, the decision to skip usually involves the student and his desires; even so, the practice is not entirely risk-free. Take the case of Benjamin Walsh, who skipped from the fourth to the seventh grade and is experiencing some mild ostracism and difficulties in algebra I, even though math has always been his strongest subject. "He professes to be happy in school, but, in retrospect, I think that it would have been better for Benjamin to skip only one grade," says his mother, Gloria Walsh. Part of Benjamin's motivation, she suspects, might have been a desire to emulate his sister, who at age sixteen is in her third year of college and found grade skipping both intellectually and socially gratifying. It's imperative that you and your teen discuss intellectual and emotional readiness—and motivation—for grade skipping, especially if he or she is thinking about skipping more than one or two grades. Remember: too much sometimes is too much.

How do parents see that teens get what they need?

Gloria Walsh's concern shows the crucial issue for parents: matching the appropriate educational option with the specific needs of your teen. That calls for you to act as the seasoned diplomat, the unflappable leader, the obliging servant, and the no-nonsense lawyer—usually all at once. In general, the model falls into the category of public relations.

Parents underestimate their power to influence the schools their teenagers attend. Because giftedness in our culture is often misunderstood, school officials and even teachers hesitate to promote programs for gifted students. So, for gifted students, parents are frequently the only advocate. If you don't make sure your teen gets the best possible education, no one will do it for you. Even if your state has the best gifted programs in the nation, your first responsibility in advocacy is for the rights of your teen.

Focusing on your teen's needs helps you to define the kinds of responses you and your school can create. Some school officials do not associate special needs with gifted students, reverting instead to the widely-held misperception that gifted students take care of themselves. Some, in fact, tend to see education of gifted students as a special privilege rather than as necessary educational responses to special needs. But if a student with a learning disability has a right to learn at the highest level possible, the same holds true for the gifted student. High ability, like low ability, creates special needs. Your job as advocate for your teen is to see that education—whatever its form—meets those needs.

Get involved with your school even before you really feel a pressing need to talk about a problem. Although parents agree that it becomes more difficult to be actively involved as children move from elementary to middle and high schools, there are still opportunities. You need to seek them out, shake the principal's hand, get to know your teen's teachers, and let them all know your concerns. For the most part, you can succeed in helping schools educate your teen, if you look upon your role as advocate also as a partnership with your school. Schools are all interested in education, and (when they admit their deepest ideals) they will welcome a partner to help them do the job of educating your special-needs teen.

But, unfortunately, sometimes you will not be heard and the school will deflect your concerns, even though your case is balanced and well thought through. Then, quite literally, it's time to call for reinforcements, and an advocacy group becomes necessary.

How do I confirm my teen's abilities?

The first step in helping your teen is to establish the facts about abilities. In many cases, making sure that your teen's needs are addressed is simply a matter of making it clear to your school exactly what those needs are. But remember, facts differ in credibility. We more easily believe something we witness ourselves than we do third-hand reports about some event. We consider rumors less seriously than we consider clearly stated judgments. We are more critical of information from someone with an interest than we are of information from a disinterested party.

Facts become useful when they are credible. And one of the most difficult problems that parents face is credibility. Let's face it: when we talk about our kids (even our teenagers) we are not always a credible bunch. We are incredibly tied to our children, and we are supremely interested in the opportunities and challenges they receive.

Paradoxically, in order to advocate for your teen credibly, sometimes you need to "remove yourself" from the situation. This is difficult when your evidence consists of your own observations, as is the case when parents discover that something is going on with their teen when problem behaviors emerge—gifted and talented students sometimes fight boredom in school by becoming disruptive or by underachieving. It is not credible to say that bad behavior is a sign of giftedness, but such behavior can be a sign that a teen and school circumstances are not well matched. Boredom, pure and simple, is a problem for highly able students, and it is a bellwether indicating that life at school is not up to your teen's needs. Meeting those needs means identifying your teen as "gifted"—and doing that credibly.

Think of identification as finding the facts of your teen's intellectual gift. Here, your evidence needs to be credible. For without evidence of your teen's intellectual gift, it is much harder to convince your school that your teen needs to be served. Evidence of that gift comes in various forms, but for it to be useful it needs to be credible *from the (often skeptical) point-of-view of the school.* Your stories and observations are useful, but they are not uniformly credible—especially if school officials or teachers do not know you personally. If you work with the school diplomatically, you may find that your observations and desires and comments will gain credibility.

Assessments of intelligence are more credible when they are standardized and professional. If you haven't done so already, a professionally administered intelligence or achievement test is a good place to start in your role as an advocate—for two, mostly unrelated, reasons: First, you learn more about your teen's abilities and you have something objective (or at least professional) and credible to talk with your school officials about. Second, the mere fact that you requested or obtained a professional assessment often gives you more credibility, because you are willing to accept another, less interested, opinion.

If your school doesn't offer intelligence testing, school counselors usually can recommend an agency or professional who can do the testing. You can also call the education department of a local college or university and ask that your teen be tested for "giftedness." In most cases, the results of a test allow you and your school to begin talking about the specific circumstances and needs of your teen. And since the results originate from the neutral territory of a testing agency or other professional, your own subjective viewpoint is not an issue.

Getting credit or advanced placement (or "skipping") for courses done at summer programs for academically talented students means that the programs and the parents need to compile and present credible facts to schools. Several summer programs offer teens the opportunity to complete regular school courses, especially in mathematics, in short summer sessions. For example, the Duke University TIP summer programs expect seventh- to tenth-grade students who are enrolled in pre-calculus mathematics to complete at least one year's worth of algebra, geometry, or functions in a three-week session—usually at least one year before the course would be offered to them back home. The track record of that program shows that students not only complete the work, but retain it and make use of it when they return to their home schools. TIP carefully substantiates every student's progress. Courses are described in great detail. Narrative evaluations from teachers, extensive testing at several points in the course, and results from a standardized End-of-Course Examination are compiled for every student completing a math course. Teachers recommend continued work back home, including placement into the next course in the mathematics sequence, review and testing, or sometimes retaking of the course.

Despite this exhaustive documentation, a few schools deny any recognition of TIP students' achievements—usually because teachers deem it incredible that anyone could master algebra or geometry in just three weeks. But for the most part, schools find the documentation useful, and they will grant placement into the next course. They are especially willing to do so when a parent contacts them beforehand in order to inform them of their teen's involvement *and* in order to ask them for guidance about how to make that involvement pay off in the following school year. In many cases, schools provide parents with certain requirements up front, and they may share policies which govern credit or placement. In any case, dialogue with schools makes it possible for schools to respond constructively at the outset rather than resort immediately to a defensive posture when parents come by with news of what their teens did during the summer.

The moral? Some schools are less likely to accept judgments that they have had no role in making. As institutions, schools often respond like individuals: They prefer to be in the loop and are not initially receptive to unanticipated demands. From the time you first consider requesting anything extraordinary for your teen, ask for help from your school. Even when no help is offered by your school, nonetheless keep your school informed about what you are doing and what you will be providing to them. Let them anticipate your requests and ideas.

Can I still talk with my teen's teacher?

Parent-teacher conferences are a simple and effective way to keep in contact. You can request a conference, or your school can request one. Sometimes the process of meeting with school officials is associated with a flurry of paperwork activity, a by-product of government regulation and oversight as well as protection in today's litigious society. Don't be dismayed by having to sign your name as many times at a school conference as you would at a real estate closing, but be vigilant about what you sign.

Before, during, and after conferences, ask questions. Before the conference, ask your teen how things are going at school, and ask for concrete examples. At the conference, be prepared to listen to the teacher and ask for any explanations of your teen's progress when necessary. Tell the teacher about anything that is happening outside of school—such as family troubles—that may be affecting your teen's classroom experience. Be willing to work with teachers and administrators to solve problems and suggest new solutions; be cooperative and positive, even if you don't agree with the ideas at first. At the first sign of educational jargon, ask for specific meanings— "What does that mean?" "How will that change and improve the situation?" "How will we know?" And, if you aren't satisfied with answers, say so, and say why you aren't satisfied. After your conference is done, follow up with questions and communications. If the conference has succeeded, it should *open* lines of communication on a less formal basis.

You'll need open lines of communication, for in working with schools, as in much of life, there's lots that can be negotiated.

What can an advocacy group do for me?

If you have exhausted your personal energy and resources, or if you want to effect bigger changes than you are able to as an individual parent, you may want to join an advocacy group. A well-respected group, known in the community, will be better able than an individual parent to convince the powers-that-be, such as school boards and legislators, that change is necessary. But a group handles individuals' cases differently than an individual parent does—and this difference profoundly changes the way that you use an advocacy group to change the circumstances of your teen.

Advocacy groups by nature focus on policies and system issues, while your individual advocacy efforts are best suited to the specific needs of your teen. Sometimes that broad focus is exactly what's needed—especially if you begin to discover in your dialogue that the school has nothing to say, so to speak. There may be no policy to support gifted students. Funds might be lacking. It could even be that school officials believe they have no gifted students in the school population, and so they have never addressed the issues of gifted education.

What applies to individual advocacy usually also applies to the group approach: Keep schools in the loop. Let your school know what you are doing and invite teachers and school officials to your meetings. Build as broad a base of support as possible from the beginning. Having a balanced group of parents and school staff will maximize your credibility—you won't be seen as just a bunch of angry parents out to cause trouble for the established order, though that perception is bound to appear as soon as your group meets controversy.

Controversy tends to accompany change, and change is exactly what an advocacy group calls for, whether the change is rescinding a decision to eliminate gifted education programs (a decision which quite effectively galvanizes parents of gifted students) or developing new programs for gifted students. It is not enough to know that change is necessary; you need to know what to change and how to change it. An advocacy group usually can begin its work by determining what opportunities, if any, currently serve gifted and talented students and how broadly and effectively they serve the students. Among the documents to look at are written school policies, budgets, reading and math scores by school, and any written school goals or plans. Indeed, your school might welcome a chance to let you know how parents can play a role in decision-making. But since a group forms a corporate voice in the dialogue with the school, expect that your dialogue will be more formal. Get things in writing—not only to build a history of interactions, but also to make sure that your messages and intentions are less likely to be misinterpreted.

Advocates for gifted education need to begin by building interest and support within a small group, then expand that interest and support to other groups. The key to successful advocacy is sustained effort. If you and your group work to achieve a small goal, and then give up on your efforts, you may miss the opportunity to gain a larger victory. The larger victory, in any case, boils down to success of your teenager in school. His or her success is the essential element, and your work as an advocate always works toward that simple end.

Sometimes you go it alone, sometimes you have the benefit (and consolation) of companionship. Whatever, your teen counts.

What to Do About Getting Ahead

AP and IB spell opportunity for teens looking to get a jump on college.

On a bright, early spring afternoon in Charlotte, North Carolina, sunlight streamed in through the windows of a large classroom as forty-seven students discussed Herman Hesse's *Siddhartha*. There wasn't much lecturing going on, the students didn't crumple under the weight of challenges to their comments, and the discussion just flowed freely. It was another day in the typical college classroom—except it was a high school. And the hands waving in the air weren't attached to college students—they belonged to a bunch of highly motivated tenth graders. They were the first students to take part in Myers Park High School's International Baccalaureate program.

It's a nice scene, but it isn't typical of America's school systems, which, in general, are under fire. Many people are saying our schools aren't preparing students adequately and that the education is too soft. Fortunately for you and your teen, there are ways of at least partially overcoming this problem by doing advanced, college-level work in the high school setting. The International Baccalaureate (IB), a relative newcomer on the American educational scene, is one such program. A similar and better-known program is the Advanced Placement Program (AP) run by The College Board, the same organization that sponsors the SAT.

Participating in either of these programs may require both you and your teen to change some of your attitudes. In foreign schools, for instance, students are often expected to bear large and demanding workloads. Mamie Heard, the coordinator of Myers Park's fledgling IB program, spent several years on the faculty of a school in Rome. "In America, we're more concerned with students having fun," she says. "Parents want their kids to enjoy their high school years." And while Heard also believes that students who are active outside the classroom are a beautiful match for programs like these, academics are really the name of the game.

What are these programs, anyway?
Advanced Placement

The AP program was established in 1955 as a way to tie academically rich high school courses with a national testing program that allows students to receive college credit for work they do in high school. Over seven thousand high schools participate in the program, and around half a million AP exams are given each year. The three-hour exams are administered near the end of the school year and are graded on a one-to-five scale. A five means the student is "extremely well-qualified"; other scores translate into "well-qualified," "qualified," "possibly qualified," and "no recommendation." The exams are straightforward in format, with a multiple choice section and a free-response essay section.

The multiple choice section is graded in SAT fashion by machine, but the essays require the human touch. This is provided by exam readers, groups of high school and college teachers specially trained by The College Board and the Educational Testing Service for the grading process. "I was impressed with how fairly the exams are graded," says Emily Warner, an AP teacher who has also served as a reader. "I am convinced that exams can be graded fairly by humans."

The College Board offers course plans and descriptions to teachers, and other organizations offer manuals designed to improve or establish AP courses. Also, to encourage professional interaction, workshops for AP teachers are available across the country.

The College Board doesn't tie specific courses to specific grade levels and instead leaves that decision to individual schools. But grade placement can be a concern if a high school offers most AP courses in the twelfth grade—that could mean problems like a course logjam or overworked students and teachers. Most schools avoid that situation by offering AP courses in at least the eleventh and twelfth grades, and some offer them as early as the tenth grade.

International Baccalaureate

Like the AP program, the International Baccalaureate Diploma program offers students high-level courses that lead to a series of examinations. Unlike AP, the IB is a comprehensive curriculum that allows its graduates to meet the requirements of educational systems in many different countries. And that's exactly where the very idea of an International Baccalaureate got its start—the practical and educational concerns of the international school setting.

The children of foreign diplomats, for instance, might attend high school in one country and college in another. Since curriculum styles vary among nations, it could be difficult for students to cross the educational borders successfully. As early as 1962, the International Schools Association began looking into the possibility of a joint social studies exam, as a first step in establishing a basic standard curriculum. Then, in 1965 the International Baccalaureate Organisation was established in Geneva, Switzerland, to administer the IB program. IBO headquarters are still in Geneva, and there are regional offices for North America, Africa and the Middle East, Asia-Pacific, Europe, and Latin America.

Despite its origins, the program is no longer valued only by the international set. Instead it's a model for vigorous education—regardless of location or travel plans—offered at about five hundred schools in over sixty countries, including more than 150 high schools in the US.

The ultimate goal of each student in the program is to earn the IB Diploma in addition to the regular high school diploma. To accomplish that, students spend their final two years of high school studying languages, sciences, mathematics, and humanities at an advanced level. From among six groups, IB students select three or four subjects to study at the "Higher Level" and two or three to study at the "Subsidiary Level." The difference in levels amounts to an extra year of study in a subject.

In addition, the program requires students to take "Theory of Knowledge," a course the IBO considers to be the key element in its educational philosophy. Theory of Knowledge is designed to let students reflect critically on the knowledge and experiences they've acquired both inside and outside the classroom, while evaluating the bases of knowledge and experience and developing their own mode of thought. It is the only course in which the final grade comes from the individual school. In addition to their coursework, students must write an Extended Essay in any subject in the IB curriculum and complete a Creativity, Action, and Service requirement.

At the end of the IB program, students sit for the international standardized exams in their six subject areas. Each exam is graded on a scale of one to seven; a minimum total of twenty-four points is required for the diploma. (Students may get bonus points for writing a great Extended Essay or performing very well in Theory of Knowledge.) About three-fourths of IB students actually earn the diploma, and those who don't get certificates for the examinations they successfully complete.

How do we get involved?

Although the AP program states no prerequisites for entering an AP class, a willingness to work hard is essential. Some schools, however, have specific requirements for enrollment. It also won't hurt matters if your teen has a good background in a subject before taking the AP class. If you're interested in AP, talk to teachers and make sure they know what's being taught in a given AP course and how your teen needs to be prepared beforehand.

The IB Diploma program officially takes only two years, but in practice the program usually takes the entire high school career. In these cases, the actual IB courses are taught in eleventh and twelfth grades, while ninth and tenth grades are "pre-IB." Pre-IB classes are by necessity academically advanced—students might need to take a course earlier than usual in order to make room for the IB sequence later on or, say, accelerate their study of a foreign language in ninth and tenth grades so they can complete five years of a foreign language by the time they graduate.

It's definitely a rigorous approach to high school, and it's possible that students can be overloaded. Help your teen think about time requirements. "It's nowhere written that students have to take six AP courses at once, and, in fact, they probably shouldn't," says Emily Warner. "Parents should help their kids decide how much is too much."

"It reaches the point where parents can't always help kids with their homework," Heard adds. "The best support parents can give is time management." It's good to think about time management before your teen gets involved. Virginia Wilson, a high school teacher who helps write AP teacher manuals, believes you should be involved in helping your teen select courses. "Don't be overbearing," she cautions. "But sit down and think through the student's program. If you were a student, what could you handle?"

Finally, don't try to provide your teen the sole motivation for participating in programs like these. "There's a big difference in a student being self-motivated and being motivated by parents," says Heard. "It's difficult for parents to provide motivation for meeting all the requirements and doing things like library research. Parents simply can't stay on top of these things all the time. If students don't have the self-motivation to accept the challenge of the program and do the best they can, they're not going to be successful."

What's the bottom line?

Any of these programs potentially offer students the chance to get college credit while they're still in high school. In the case of AP, students earn college credit by taking the national exam in their AP subject or subjects. Credit policies vary among the two thousand colleges and universities that accept AP exam scores. Scores of three or better usually merit some sort of credit, but the most competitive colleges and universities typically only award credit for scores of four and five. The actual amount of credit awarded also varies, with some colleges awarding one quarter or one semester class credit and others awarding credit for three quarters or even a full year. At some institutions, students receive credit only if they complete an advanced course in the same field as the AP examination.

Since the IB program is less common, not all American colleges and universities have prepared official policies for dealing with IB students, but about three hundred colleges have. Most of those stated policies are similar in content: The "typical" policy grants up to two credits per Higher level exam with a score of five or higher. The most competitive schools, however, offer credit only for scores of six or seven, which Heard says are difficult to get. Those colleges and universities that don't have official IB policies work with students on a case-by-case basis. For credit purposes, IB students can also opt to take the AP exams.

No matter what the policy, credit can obviously mean early

graduation, and for students who are headed for graduate school, the possibility of getting there sooner may be a big attraction. But early graduation is not always a reality. One study released by The College Board showed that only three percent of all AP students graduate college early. In other words, students can use the credits to get their undergraduate degrees early, but they don't have to exercise that option.

This doesn't mean the AP program is useless, because saving money may be the crudest way to view it—the underlying value of the AP program is that it's an educational opportunity and challenge. Emily Warner believes college credit is the least important concern. "For my students," she says, "AP US history is the first course in which they're intellectually on their own.

"I'M TELLING YOU SON, YOU EITHER FISH OR CUT BAIT!"

Doing the work is really its own reward."

The IB is also more an educational advantage than a way to save money on college tuition. As a comprehensive curriculum, the IB definitely emphasizes the interrelatedness of the coursework. But with its international flair, the IB also emphasizes the inter-relatedness of different cultures. In essence, the program wants to educate the total person, so that students will be able to get along well in an increasingly global community.

Heard believes this multiculturalism is the biggest advantage of the IB. She explains how three local business experts addressed her economics class and told the students that, in order to be successful, they needed to bring to the job market certain skills like a foreign language and the ability to work and think with diversity. "Anybody can get a diploma from a college," says Heard. "Students who think globally, who are able to understand other cultures, and who are diverse in the way they approach things, will ultimately be successful."

Finally, don't overlook the benefits of these programs' names when it comes time for your teen to apply to college. Admissions officials almost always look favorably on students who have been in these programs, but not necessarily because AP and IB students learn so much. Students who get involved in these programs are showing a willingness to stretch their boundaries and take advantage of every opportunity available to them. Colleges like that.

What should we be concerned about?

There's a lot to be said for simply enrolling in an AP course. There's also a lot to be said for actually taking the exam. In fact, when students don't take the AP exams, they may be doing themselves a disservice—and the blame for that may rest either on students or on school officials. Donna Rogers, a former AP student, recalls that her high school faculty recommended that she and her classmates not take the AP biology exam. Their reasoning? The students were not well-prepared. Students are usually unsure about how they might stack up against a national examination, so a warning that they're not prepared is likely to catch their attention.

Of course, when high school officials encourage students not to take the AP exams, something is wrong. After completing an AP class, students should be prepared for the exam; if they're not, then the school hasn't done its job. Warner states it more plainly: "It's a sin if a school tells a student not to take the exam." She reminds administrators that The College Board doesn't judge high schools by the scores their students receive on the exam.

Always encourage your teen to take the AP exam. They have nothing to lose (except the exam fee, if the school doesn't pay for it) and everything to gain. Donna Rogers listened to school officials' advice and decided not to take the exam, but several of her classmates gave it a shot. None scored below a four.

As a program tied to a national examination, AP has also been criticized for the possibility of having teachers teach to the test, rather than actively exploring all areas of a topic. While this leaves the college credit benefit of AP unharmed, the educational benefit is diminished. AP teachers, however, put little stock in such criticisms. They claim that the exams are predictable only by their format, not by specific content, and that the essay portion of the exams requires students to organize and think through complex matters. These skills, they say, can only be taught by giving students a thorough learning experience in their coursework.

"It's a wonderful test to teach to," says Warner. "Students can't bluff their way through the test—they have to learn something in class. If you've taught a student to write and have gotten the student to do some critical thinking, what's wrong with teaching to that test?"

Some of these same criticisms can be levelled at the IB, but the fact that the IB is a comprehensive program—a fact that brings so many benefits—also brings a different sort of drawback. Quite simply, students run the risk of feeling isolated from the rest of the school. "Students feel as though they're in this huge public high school, yet they're in classes with the same students all day," says Heard. "They feel it limits them in being part of the school." Worry or not, though, it doesn't have to be the truth. "We do want them to be well-rounded," Heard continues. "The students who are most successful in the program are those who have become very involved in the school itself."

Another problem IB students may face has to do with the diploma's foreign language requirement. The purpose of the requirement is to expose students to another culture and to allow them to communicate with that culture. But Heard feels that some students, due to their location, may have problems becoming immersed in a foreign language. "That's a major drawback, not so much of the students as their background," she says.

Do these programs vary from school to school?

"You start off with a qualified teacher," says Warner. "A school should have its best faculty involved in the program and should get some guidance from The College Board, which offers good bibliographies and teaching strategies. That should mean there's not as much diversity in the quality of the program from school to school."

But there can actually be lots of diversity. While the quality of the programs themselves is high, the strength of a program is affected by the administrative aspects of the program, which vary from school to school. One such issue is grade-weighting—the practice of assigning more value to a grade received in an advanced course than a grade received in a regular course. So an A in an AP class might count five points toward the GPA, a B might count four (the same as an A in a regular course), and so on.

In some high schools, grade–weighting has helped the AP program by bringing in applications from students who otherwise would not have applied to the program. But weighted grades have actually diluted the AP program at other high schools. After her school system began weighting grades, says Warner, students who shouldn't have been in AP put themselves there. "They thought that if they got a C, it would be no problem, since they

AP Courses and Exams Available

Art History

Studio Art—General Portfolio; Drawings

Biology

Chemistry

Computer Science—A; AB

Economics—Macro; Micro

English—Language and Composition; Literature and Composition

French—Language; Literature

German Language

Government and Politics— United States; Comparative

History—European; United States

Latin—Vergil

Mathematics—Calculus AB; Calculus BC

Music Theory

Physics—B; C

Psychology

Spanish—Language; Literature

IB Subject Areas by Group

Language A/Literature

World Literature

Language B/Modern Foreign Languages

Individuals and Societies/ Social Studies

History

Geography

Economics

Philosophy

Psychology

Social Anthropology

Organization and Management Studies

Experimental Sciences

Chemistry

Biology

Physics

Environmental Systems and Design Technology

Mathematics

Mathematics with Further Mathematics

Mathematics and Computing

Mathematical Studies

Sixth Subject/Electives

Art/Design

Music

Computing Studies

Classical Languages

History and Culture of the Islamic World

A second subject from the social studies or sciences group

A third modern language

A school-based syllabus approved by the IB

would get the same quality points as if they'd gotten a B. Their grade point averages wouldn't suffer, and college admission boards would think they were wonderful because they had taken AP." The result was students who were unable or unwilling to do the work.

Since AP courses are designed to present work at the college level, it's not surprising that The College Board recommends criteria for selecting students to participate in the program. Some of the criteria they suggest are:

- parental support of the student
- motivation and commitment to completing the course
- understanding what's expected in an AP course
- appropriate reading and writing skills
- good PSAT scores
- teacher recommendations
- completion of prerequisite courses
- solid overall GPA
- strong past performance in the particular subject area.

The International Baccalaureate Organisation makes no official recommendation about who should be admitted as an IB student, but one high school in Florida offers the following selection criteria for pre-IB:

- 3.0 GPA in seventh and eighth grades (on a 4.0 scale)
- composite score of at least the eighty-fifth percentile on the Comprehensive Test of Basic Skills or its equivalent
- sample essay
- teacher recommendations
- motivation as demonstrated by excellent attendance and exemplary conduct.

High schools don't always use criteria like these for the IB program—or any criteria at all. One school in Indiana allows students to select themselves for the program. They are required neither to have participated in any gifted or talented classes nor to have achieved certain GPAs or standardized test scores. Once the program is carefully explained to the students, they are free to enroll if they so desire.

The same sort of dilution that sometimes goes hand-in-hand with grade-weighting may also happen if a school doesn't use an application procedure for the program or if a school uses an application procedure but isn't willing to deny students access to the program. Ideally, the only qualification for these programs is a willingness to work hard, but students who aren't willing are signing up. And if advanced classes enroll students who can't do the work, then everyone in the class—gifted students included—suffers. It's difficult for teachers to teach any faster than their slowest students can learn.

Another factor that might cause quality to fluctuate is school resources. Consider, for instance, course offerings—not every school has the faculty and facilities necessary to offer every course in either program. That's not unusual, and it's not a problem. "You can tailor the program to the strengths and weaknesses of your school," says Heard.

Our school doesn't offer these programs. What can we do about it?

According to Warner, you should approach your local school board with the idea. But you and the school board alike need to understand that there is money involved. The school board should be willing to send AP teachers to a workshop, which may cost several hundred dollars per teacher. They also need to invest in textbooks and additions to the school library's collection—maybe as much as several thousand dollars worth, depending on what the library already has in place.

Getting the IB program started at a school is an involved process. According to Mamie Heard, the application itself is nearly two inches thick. Essentially, each school applying for the program must present itself on the application and convince the

International Baccalaureate Organisation that the school has the faculty, facilities, and students necessary to support the program. The application procedure also includes visits to established IB schools to get a real feel for the program, reviews by representatives from the IB program both in the US and abroad, and teacher training workshops. Finally, the school receives a decision from the IBO, along with instructions for what improvements need to be made, such as upgrading lab or library facilities.

Good books are a necessary resource for any advanced student, and parents can help with this investment. Advanced classes tend to be like college classes, in that there is a required reading list in addition to the textbook. Public schools can't require students to buy these books; that's why such a heavy investment in the school library may be necessary. Teachers can encourage their students to buy the books, but the decision rests with students and parents.

Which program is better?

Both the AP and the IB are excellent programs, offering high-quality work in high school. But they are clearly different. "There is no such thing as an AP diploma," says Heard. In other words, AP students can pick and choose which classes they want to take. IB students don't have that option. For Heard, that's a significant advantage of the International Baccalaureate. "A student who had graduated from the IB program in Florida came down from her college to talk to our students. Her friends who had not been through the IB were stressed out and were having to adjust to college. But she felt it was just a natural progression, coming from the IB."

"There are advantages to both," says Virginia Wilson. "When you buy into the International Baccalaureate, you buy into a program. When you buy into Advanced Placement, you buy into a course. Students decide which AP courses they want to take and which ones they don't. The two programs are different in their approach."

If you have the luxury of choosing between programs at your local high school, consider yourself lucky for having these challenges at your teen's disposal and choose carefully between them. If your teen has access to only one of these programs, take advantage of it—even if it's a matter of only one or two AP courses—and think about working for expansion. And if your school has neither of these programs, then by all means encourage your school board to look into them.

What to Do About Other Educational Options

If your teen isn't thoroughly challenged in school, opportunities outside the classroom can renew excitement for learning.

Maggie Swanson was a high-achieving seventh grader—three years ahead of her peers in math, reading on a twelfth grade level, and excited about playing the violin and learning French in junior high. Two weeks before she was to begin seventh grade, she moved with her family from a university town to a smaller community, where she experienced both cultural and educational shock. Even had the curriculum in her new school offered orchestra, foreign language, or more advanced math, being thirteen in an academically apathetic, indifferent new peer group was more than she wanted to fight. She began to hide her intelligence and misbehave in class in order to be accepted. As if the hormonal upheaval and peer pressure of puberty are not overwhelming enough, other factors conspire every day to cause bright kids like Maggie to lose their early-developed passion for learning. Often it isn't what, where, or with whom students are taught, but *how* they are taught that helps derail the learning process.

For example, standard secondary school curriculum compartmentalizes knowledge into neat, achievable units such as "Algebra 1," or "US History," as though all knowledge fits into finite, easily mastered units. This means that rather than creating windows through which students see how much is out there to learn, we teach students from inside stifling windowless boxes. These teaching methods stem from collective adult wisdom and good intentions. We know that students need to "master the basics" in order to have a foundation for the complexities of higher education and what, from our perspective, is the real world. But from an adolescent perspective, memorized facts and formulas don't challenge capabilities and seem to have no bearing on life outside the classroom.

Many teenagers who *want* to be challenged are coddled in the classroom until college when they learn to process information rather than simply regurgitate it. Often by that time, as in Maggie's case, the passion and energy once put into learning has been less constructively redirected. "Teenagers are rotting on the vine," says Brian Hopewell, Director of Admissions at Simon's Rock College of Bard. "They don't control the educational system—adults do. And as long as the adults who control the system think learning needs to be infantilized, it's going to keep happening." Indeed, many students thrive within regular classrooms with talented teachers, but far too many gifted students *need* a more powerful educational experience than their present school environment affords.

Resuscitating or redirecting your teenager's passion and energy is only one reason to look beyond the traditional secondary school for your teen's education. There are many good reasons to look into special schools, summer programs, competitions, and other opportunities for what is referred to as "enrichment and acceleration." There may also be many good reasons why a particular opportunity might not be the right one for you and your teen. As Hopewell puts it, "These programs can save a student's life, but they can also put him in hot water."

There are some options for talented students beyond the traditional school setting and some less positive factors, or "hot water," to consider when making decisions. But there are also a few more general ways enrichment and acceleration might help to save a student who is, if not academically derailed, maybe needing just a little more forward momentum or divergence than school has to offer.

My teen is gifted, taking challenging courses, and making excellent grades. What more could she need?

Sometimes even in the most rigorous high schools, gifted teens are bored because the type of challenge they meet in school is in the area they are most gifted. They may also need to be challenged in an area they feel deficient, or they may be gifted in an area their school curriculum does not touch. Sometimes in our zeal to encourage mathematical and verbal talent, we overlook the many other talents a young person may *want* to develop. A teenager who is gifted in math and labeled by his peers as a "math nerd" may have a deep longing, and hence an undiscovered talent, for performing on stage or shooting a basketball. But the expectations of his peer group, and sometimes his family, may inhibit him from taking a risk and trying out for the school play.

Put this teen in a new environment free from the expectations of peers and family, and one of two scenarios is likely to occur. One—he pursues his dream and falls flat on his face. Or two—a star is born. Even if he fails, the cost of failure at this age is lower than later in life, and lessons learned early can be beneficial in the long run. Whatever the outcome, the new environment, complete with new peer group, has allowed him the freedom to pursue a dream and to explore his own limits and capabilities.

A new learning environment may offer a teen like our "math nerd" an outlet for expressing a previously untested gift, or it may offer new ideas for how disparate talents might be combined in a career. For example, students in many residential summer programs are offered career seminars or internships in which they see firsthand how a love of chemistry and studio art can be combined in a career as a museum conservator, or how a career in electrical engineering can combine musical and mathematical talent into research in music synthesis.

The key to a young person's (or any person's) productivity

"SO WHAT IF HE'S NOT POTTY TRAINED? HE'S GIFTED."

may lie chiefly in his or her measure of what Harvard psychologist Howard Gardner calls *"intra*personal intelligence," or self-knowledge, and *"inter*personal intelligence," or the ability to understand and thus effectively motivate, lead, cooperate with, or care for others. While a student may indeed be "gifted" with a measure of intrapersonal or interpersonal intelligence, Gardner believes these two capacities develop and strengthen over time more than do other intellectual gifts. However, they are not likely to blossom miraculously as students sit facing the front of a classroom passively absorbing knowledge bestowed upon them by one human being. The challenge of new people and situations, or the same old people thrust into competition together, is more likely to bring about growth and self-discovery than is the lack of interaction within most classrooms.

An environment in which a student is challenged and stretched by the talent of similarly gifted peers, the enthusiasm of gifted teachers, and the high expectations of a selective institution can tremendously impact a teen's self awareness and ability to interact effectively with others, in addition to providing an intense academic experience. But these intense academic experiences come complete with lots of risks and unknowns for the parents involved.

What lies beyond school?

Residential summer programs can be an excellent opportunity for a teen to test the waters away from Mom and Dad and to try out a new course, a new place, new friends, and sometimes even a new personality! And there is a mind-reeling array of opportunities out there. There are sea camps, space camps, computer, government, engineering, science, fine arts, and math camps. There are programs that offer college credit, a taste of college, leadership skills, rapid acceleration, intensive language study, cultural tours, comparative environmental studies, archaeological digs, astronomical exploration, career exploration, training in writing, thinking, research, and the list goes on. They come in institutes, treks, adventures, academies, sessions, workshops, experiences, odysseys, and even a lyceum or two. But basically they have at least one thing in common—they bring together a peer group with a common interest in acquiring knowledge.

Of course, degrees of enthusiasm among teens vary. Some go to such experiences just to get away from Mom and Dad, and others go because Mom and Dad didn't give them a choice or gave them a wholly unappealing alternative. But those kids generally blend in with the group and often catch the contagious enthusiasm. Seldom do program administrators tolerate disruptive students who taint the experience for others.

The benefits talented students gain from residential summer programs are to a great extent the same as those gained from an academic year boarding experience, as are many of the negative considerations. The programs tend to foster close friendships with like-minded peers and offer curricula unavailable at home, a higher caliber of students and faculty, and teachers with high expectations for their students. By the same token, programs vary widely in terms of duration, cost, residential supervision and support, nature of the classroom experience, and selectivity and diversity of students and faculty, among other factors.

One significant difference between school and many summer programs is that the summer experience is short enough that students don't lose their momentum, and just long enough that students have an intense academic experience without real-life considerations encroaching on their fun. Obviously this quality varies with the length and nature of the program, but residential summer programs tend to be mountaintop experiences. While mountaintops are wonderful and exhilarating, they also have downhill slopes.

A teen can return from the mountaintop inspired and motivated, but returning to a regular classroom and an uninspired peer group can be somewhat of a wet sponge on the fires of enthusiasm. This can be especially true of programs that attempt to allow students to experience college. Rebecca Shannon, a high school senior from Topeka, Kansas, has attended multiple summer programs, most recently attending Duke University's PreCollege Program. "When I got home, high school was awful! I missed the caliber of students, the class discussions, and teachers who could make you work."

Susan Shannon is the mother of both Rebecca and Princeton senior Alan, who also attended several residential summer programs. She feels that while both Rebecca and Alan had wonderful experiences, "Kids should be taught that life isn't always a bowl of cherries. These programs would serve students well to create an awareness of problems they will face in college. By sheltering students from reality, they create unreasonable expectations for college." Susan also relates Alan's experiences at one program where residential restrictions and requirements were so rigid that "mandatory fun" cut into time he would rather have spent studying or relaxing.

Susan is more aware than many parents of the dilemma program administrators face: on the one hand they want parents to trust children to their care, and on the other they want to offer students a significant growth experience. Parents should carefully examine a program's philosophies regarding participants' lives outside the classroom, particularly in light of freedoms you may not wish your teen to have, or realities you would rather he or she not face just yet.

The Shannon family could convince even the most bitter skeptic that residential summer programs are a positive, life-changing event for the whole family. Rebecca also attended three summers of Duke's Young Writers' Camp and two programs at Northwestern—a biology course in the Summer Program for Academically Talented Adolescents and a five-week theater course at the National High School Institute. This may sound like overkill, but summer burnout has never been an issue with Rebecca: "I have had the most incredible times bonding with friends—the summer at Northwestern was the most amazing time of my life!" Susan says her phone bills and the number of letters Rebecca sends out testify to the strength of summer friendships.

While friendships are of immense importance to teenagers, the academic experience can be equally life-changing. Rebecca, who is now in the midst of college decision making, says she wrote about her learning experience at Duke in her admissions essays. "I learned how to think at Duke. My classes taught me that I could no longer simply memorize facts and quote research books, but I could criticize literature and make valid arguments. I was turned on to knowledge, and I learned how much was really out there to learn!"

But what happens when summer is over?

Academic competitions are one way students who go away for the summer can keep the academic fires burning when they return home. The same can be true of students for whom leaving home for lengthy programs or boarding school is not a possibility. Academic competitions provide many of the same benefits in terms of academic challenge and enthusiastic peers.

Linda Yu's sixteen-year-old son Eric got a perfect SAT score while still in grade school. He is currently dually enrolled in high school and college but has been both academically and socially ready to leave home for some time now. "I have probably kept him at home longer than he has wanted, but home life and the values we instill at home are too important. It's not that he can't obtain the same values elsewhere, but we are in no hurry to send him away. Once he leaves, he leaves." Linda is wholly in favor of longer residential experiences in some instances. "The camaraderie involved when everyone is striving for the same thing is very important. Not everyone has the opportunities for academic challenge locally that we have had. If our situation were different, we might consider the sacrifice of home life."

Most of Eric's present academic challenges come from competition. He has participated in numerous math, science, and music contests and was a winner in the 1993 Westinghouse Science Talent Search. Linda feels that competition bolsters Eric's achievements. "Even in defeat he is inspired to do better and better. He has learned to manage himself and put things in perspective." It can also be no small thing to win scholarship money in a competition rather than spending money saved for college on summer programs. The top winner in the Westinghouse program receives a forty thousand dollar college scholarship, and forty finalists win a minimum of one thousand dollars each.

Many of the benefits of competition are somewhat less tangible than cash. "I made friends from all over the state," says Michael McKinnis, whose high school JETS (Junior Engineering and Technical Society) team was number one in the state of Illinois. "Studying for competitions each month also improved my competence in my regular school subjects. Now that I'm in college, I realize that competition helped prepare me for the kind of rigor to expect here."

Another type of competition that is rapidly gaining popularity because it emphasizes the learning process is the creative problem solving competition. Odyssey of the Mind (OM) is a competition as well as an organization which provides sample curricula to member schools to teach creative problem solving. Competing teams are given five challenges that have many possible solutions. The challenges, such as building and demonstrating a vehicle powered by a piston rising on a hydraulic jack, require the application of technical principles. Carole Micklus, Executive Director of OM Association, Inc. says, "It's easier to grasp a principle when it's applied in a skill setting. Students don't have to ask 'Why am I learning this?' Not only does research become real, control over the outcome and the learning process is in the students' own hands."

The program strictly forbids adults to help, thus allowing learning to become important to the students. Odyssey of the Mind is a wonderful illustration of what happens in acceleration and enrichment programs that allow students to benefit from the influence of adults but not to the extent that their *learning* environment is completely under the control of adults.

What if my teenager needs a more radical change of environment?

In some instances, summer programs and extracurricular enrichment help to create a greater need for change. Students may exhaust local opportunities for enrichment or accelerate in some subjects far beyond their current grade level. These exceptional students may need a more radical change of educational environment to cultivate or maintain their gifts. Such a radical change might be found in an academic-year boarding experience, or perhaps even early college entrance.

Early college entrance would seem the most radical option, or at least one which many parents would consider only under somewhat extreme circumstances. Many colleges and universities will *consider* admitting a student after the junior year if, in addition to normal admissions considerations, the student can demonstrate having depleted the educational resources available in his or her high school. Many institutions, however, are reluctant to consider admitting younger students because they can't realistically make provisions for the students' special developmental needs.

Simon's Rock College of Bard, Mary Baldwin College's Program for the Exceptionally Gifted (PEG), the University of Washington's Early Entrance Program, and a handful of other institutions offer early entrance programs specifically catering to students who are ready academically and emotionally to enter college earlier than the conventional age of eighteen. According to Brian Hopewell of Simon's Rock, entering college as early as fifteen or sixteen is not as radical an option as one might think. "Only in the twentieth century has the age of eighteen been a college entrance standard. Readiness should be the mark, not age." Mary Baldwin's program considers some young women ready after the eighth grade. Students enter most other early admission programs after the tenth or eleventh grade.

Hopewell feels that early college entrance can save the talented student who is a minimalist, doing as little as possible for as much credit as possible. These students, although high achievers, are not reaching their full potential and are in danger of losing the motivation to use their academic talents.

Allison Young, PEG's assistant director for program development, agrees with Hopewell on the merits of early admission programs but advises parents of high-achieving young people to try to meet their needs at home first. "Pursuing local options for enrichment and acceleration is far less disruptive than shipping a teen off, in some instances across the country. A decision to send a student to college several years ahead of her peers impacts everyone, siblings included, and ultimately may leave you with an eighteen-year-old college graduate on your hands."

Sending a teen to college early is a difficult choice for parents, but one which might be made easier when you consider the choices your teen already has to make. Gifted teens often have to choose between what Hopewell calls "numbing conformity" and being true to their abilities. "Young people who are genuinely interested in education and ideas are often considered profoundly uncool. They are forced to make a choice between demonstrating their competence and being part of a group."

Even in a college or university town where dual enrollment may be possible, the decision to send your teen to an early admission program may indeed be the right one. Dual enrollment at a local college provides only older friends, whereas early entrance programs provide a peer group which your student may desperately need. The common focus, high energy level, and intensity among a peer group in an early admission program can act as a sort of particle accelerator, bringing highly charged particles together to produce powerful results.

The benefits a student receives both emotionally and intellectually may outweigh such family considerations as disruption of home life. And then again they may not! In general, early admission programs provide excellent residential support for their students, but philosophies vary somewhat as to the freedoms and responsibilities given to students. In some instances, students are treated not much differently than other college students are treated. In other cases, supervision is more thorough, and expectations regarding study hours, service hours, or attendance at other types of functions are much higher.

Differences in philosophy are also found in the classroom. Some institutions offer transitional courses to prepare their students for critical thinking and other aspects of college. Other institutions only accept students who they feel have exhibited readiness for all aspects of college work. Still others simply place students in classes with college-aged undergraduates while maintaining separate residential activities and structures. Because some highly charged young "particles" are more volatile than others, parents considering early admission programs should consider their teens' residential as well as academic needs.

Like early college entrance programs, many prep schools offer challenges and rewards in terms of rigor and depth of curriculum, talent and diversity of student population and instructors, and richness of residential life and support. In some cases prep schools even exceed early college entrance programs. The primary reason for considering a prep school is that it isn't always advantageous for a student to be chronologically far out of step with his or her peers. Certainly admission to college as much as two or three years early shouldn't be considered unless your teen is already far ahead academically.

What about other options in my state?

Some regions of the country do not have a tradition of prep school education, but that is changing, as states are beginning to develop state-supported, residential high schools which usually focus on certain academic disciplines, like math and science. In fact, state-supported, public, residential high schools for eleventh and twelfth graders are cropping up all over the country, following the success of the North Carolina School of Science and Mathematics (NCSSM). The level of funding varies by institution and, in some instances, costs are considerable. But in several states, the schools are considered public magnet schools and are entirely free of charge.

Well, maybe not entirely. In some states, students are required to perform work service hours on campus and community service at home over school breaks in return for the state's support for tuition, fees, and room and board (a thirteen thousand dollar per year per student gift in North Carolina in 1992-93). Community service hours in some instances are graded and must be completed satisfactorily before a student returns for his or her senior year. Generally sixty hours of community service are required, and in the case of a student working to save for college, this can be an added strain, because saving for college comes from a paid, after-school, after-community-service job.

The service experience, however, can tremendously benefit the student, the community, and the family. Doug Gray, assistant principal at NCSSM, feels that the experience of doing landscape work, serving in a cafeteria, or performing office tasks gives the students a sense of community, responsibility, and ownership of the educational experience. As Gray puts it, "In their home schools, students are like passengers on an airplane. Here they are the pilots."

Service hours are only one way the learning experience at a residential high school extends beyond the classroom. Experiences like doing laundry or cleaning a toilet reveal—sometimes startlingly—the mundane realities that adults (and especially parents) face. Beyond that, teens experience living within a budget and living with a roommate. Some teens have no problem dealing with these new-found facets of independence. Then again, some teenagers flounder under the same circumstances. Even with outstanding support systems in place to help students adjust, approximately eight percent of NCSSM's students leave every year.

NCSSM students are screened rigorously both for academic readiness and personal maturity through testing, recommendations, and interviews, as are students seeking admission to any of the public residential high schools. But no amount of screening can predict with one hundred percent certainty how a student will cope with new levels of independence and responsibility. The same is true of any first-time-away-from-home experience, whether it is a short-term summer program or college. But even failure to adjust to living away sometimes leads to positive self-discovery and redirection. Better to leave high school to return home than to leave college, when the alternatives may not be as appealing.

Aside from the boarding experience, one advantage these high schools have over local public schools is curricular breadth. A student who has exhausted the science offerings of his local high school may be able to choose from as many as thirty-two science courses at NCSSM. He can also choose an independent study with a faculty member on campus or a mentorship with a professional at any of a number of outstanding research facilities nearby. The same is true almost across the board. Virtually no hometown high school, public or private, has the diversity of educational resources that are available at state-supported residential high schools.

Tina Cheevers, a junior at the Indiana Academy for Science, Mathematics, and Humanities, came to the Academy from one of the best high schools in her state. "However," she says, "the level of education is far greater here. There is a much wider variety of classes, and the level of discussion in the classroom is intense. Both the students and the teachers go through a rigorous selection process to get here." As Tina points out, the selectivity of such a school environment allows students to interact with equally talented and enthusiastic peers and to learn from professionals at the top of their fields.

Selectivity of institutions varies, both with regard to faculty and students. Faculty are generally selected in regional, if not national, searches, and in most instances they hold masters or doctoral degrees. The high quality of student populations, availability of grant money, and, in some cases, proximity to major research institutions have helped to make these schools appealing to highly trained, enthusiastic, and competent teachers.

Students are selected without exception through rigorous screening processes. However, the actual selection processes vary widely. In general, each institution seeks top students from its state, but other factors may enter into the process. Because they are public, some institutions must select a certain number of students from each congressional district or from among otherwise designated regions of the state. Other institutions admit applicants with less regard to diversifying the student population or to serving a wider cross-section of school districts. Admissions policies may not seem to be important considerations, but they can make a considerable difference in the character of the student body, the breadth of courses offered, and thus what students take away from the experience.

Expectations for admission may also change when a student is in competition for one of only a few spaces offered within a home school district. Students who have had more educational advantages may be at somewhat of a disadvantage in admissions when regional or district quotas are involved. By the same token, in the absence of such considerations, students probably will not gain as rich a residential experience from studying with peers who are all from similar backgrounds.

ADDITIONAL RESOURCES

1992 Educational Opportunity Guide: A Directory of Programs for the Gifted. The Duke University Talent Identification Program. Published annually.

Contests for Students: All You Need to Know to Enter and Win 600 Contests. Ed. Mary Ellen Snodgrass, 1991. Gale Research, Inc.

The Creative Spirit (Companion to the 1992 PBS Television Series), by Daniel Goleman, Paul Kaufman, Michael Ray. Dutton Books—Division of Penguin Books, USA.

NASSP National Advisory List of Contests and Activities. National Association of Secondary School Principals (US). Published annually.

Handbook of Private Schools: An Annual Descriptive Survey of Independent Education, and *Guide to Summer Camps and Programs,* by Porter Sargent.

Science Service Directory of Student Science Training Programs for Precollege Students. Published annually. Ed. Science Service Staff.

Peterson's Summer Opportunities for Kids and Teenagers 1993, 10th edition.

Peterson's Private Secondary Schools 1993-1994, 14th edition.

Summer Options for Teenagers. Ed. Cindy Ware, 1990. Arco.

Directory of Programs for Gifted Children, 1991. Graduate Group.

National Association of Independent Schools. *Boarding School Directory 1993.* Free.

Do specialized schools give students an edge in college admissions?

Tina Cheevers believes that when it comes time for college applications she will have an edge she wouldn't have had if she had stayed at home for all of high school. To some extent this is true. Students who are genuinely interested in ideas and learning and who seek academic challenge aggressively have an edge over students who may be equally talented but have done nothing to further themselves academically. However, nothing guarantees that Tina will have her choice of schools or that people will be knocking down her door with scholarship offers.

According to Tamara Siler, Assistant Director of Admissions at Rice University, "The edge these students often have is related to the high quality of the academic programs available to them. The instruction they receive in science and mathematics is excellent preparation for highly selective universities, and these schools produce students with outstanding SAT and ACT scores. On the downside, though, the rigor of their curriculum means that some students spend such concentrated time on academics that they have little social or extracurricular involvement. Sometimes these students lack the leadership qualities and well-roundedness they need to stand out among an extremely competitive applicant pool."

Parents should request a school profile, not only to familiarize themselves with the caliber of the school, but to help gear their expectations for things like grade reports. The whiz kid who has always come home with straight As and been ranked at the top of the class may create shock waves by coming home with Bs or Cs and no class rank at all. Stiffer competition and higher standards come hand-in-hand with that great new peer group. Many selective schools don't rank their students because they feel it is counterproductive to thrust top students into the middle or bottom of a more selective heap.

State-supported residential high schools, early college admissions programs, academic competitions, and residential summer

Final Considerations

in science competitions...

❶ Beware of inexperienced or unknowledgeable mentors—misinformation can lead to disaster!

in special schools...

❷ Is specialized curriculum offered at the expense of college preparation?

❸ Remember to consider residential and personal needs and readiness as well as academic needs.

in general...

❹ Weigh the cost of the investment against possible benefits, and consider less expensive, high quality alternatives.

❺ When possible, consult a school counselor or independent educational counselor. They can provide objective opinions and hard-to-find information.

❻ Read everything that has been written about a particular program, *especially the fine print!*

programs are only a few of the opportunities available to bright students. There are also specialized non-boarding magnet schools, experimental schools, and short-term, local enrichment programs available in many communities. You only need to look.

What to Do About Travel

**With the right planning, you can teach
your teen a thing or two on the road.**

"I don't know how it is for other families," Dot Meyer says,
"but for Bob and I the family trip is a lot like having relatives over
for Thanksgiving. Lots to plan, lots of fretting. And then lots of
fun with a little nagging and headache mixed in." Bob and Dot
Meyer have three children, all about evenly spaced and split
between elementary, middle and high schools. They have regu-
larly taken family vacations, sometimes just to relatives for
Thanksgiving, but they have tried to make their trips worthwhile
for the kids. And they have even taken their children out of school
for short periods when they need more time than a school break
allows. "The kids learn a good deal on the road that they can't

get in school," Bob says. "A ship harbor or the Golden Gate
Bridge is different in a book than it is right before your eyes.
We think the kids have some real advantages because of our
travel together."

Bob is probably right, and he certainly has plenty of precedence to cite for his view. Long ago, travel and education were
linked so closely that they were virtually inseparable. Sir Francis
Bacon summed it up: "Travel, in the younger sort, is a part of
Education." The old connection of going somewhere and learning something persists and may even be growing stronger. *Travel
& Leisure* commissioned the Louis Harris and Associates polling
organization to ask travelers about their expectations and attitudes.
The poll found that travelers' attitudes will lead them to places
where they can be enriched educationally or culturally. Figuratively
speaking, the casinos of Las Vegas may not have the draw in the
'90s that they had in the '80s. The '90s traveler has other bottom lines in mind, and one of the reasons for travel is educational enrichment.

What applies to the individual traveler also applies to family travelers, for the *Travel & Leisure* poll found that some of the
shift in travel interests may result from generally tighter finances
in the 1990s. Tight finances often are the norm for families, so
travel that encourages learning makes double sense. It makes cash
go further; it helps the kids make the most of their educations.

The *Travel & Leisure* study provides an "adult" and, perhaps, a generalized view of 1990s travel. Another study, The
Hyatt Report on Vacationing Teens, looks at the attitudes and
travel habits of teens from twelve to seventeen. The survey sam-
pled only teens from families with household income in excess of
$50,000. The study outlines five categories which describe teens'
attitudes toward vacation, and their names practically describe
themselves: Hot Shots; Young and Restless; All-Americans; Moody
Blues; and Lone Rangers.

All-Americans and Moody Blues almost evenly split the majority of teens—with 27% and 28%, respectively. But their sample

"MAYBE WE SHOULD DO MORE AS A FAMILY!"

sizes are about the only thing that's similar between the two categories. All-Americans are parent- and travel-friendly. They are family-oriented, considerate, take along books and cameras, and count religion and school important in the "regular," non-traveling life. Opposite these happy teens are the Moody Blues—whose name describes them quite well. They are moody. They are blue. They are the teens who need to be dragged to the car or to the next sightseeing stop. They prefer the motel room to the Air and Space Museum. They say that their parents don't understand them, which is probably true, since some of their moping behavior seems inexplicable on vacation.

Lone Rangers, Hot Shots, and the Young and Restless teens make up the rest of the teen profiles in the Hyatt Report. Lone Rangers are the smallest of these three groups (12% of the total sample). They come from small families, have a good deal of money to spend, and often have their own hotel rooms. They do things on their own while on vacation, like going to movies or rid-

ing bikes. Young and Restless teens (20% of sample) are not all
that enthusiastic about traveling with Mom and Dad, and they'll
let them know it. The report says that Young and Restless are
usually male and "full of normal teen rebellion." If your teen is
Young and Restless, keep an eye on him. He might try to wander off to make his own fun. With the remaining 13% of the sample, Hot Shots have a name that sounds more worrisome than their
description warrants. They are athletic and independent teen
travelers, who often take trips with friends rather than with their
parents. For them, vacations mean freedom—freedom which
they have bought with their own money, too. They often have
part-time jobs, and the authors of the report consider Hot Shots
more mature than teens in the other groups.

Where to go?

As the *Travel & Leisure* and Hyatt reports suggest, everyone
has an agenda for the family vacation, and so planning it is stressful, especially if your teen is one of the Moody Blues. Dad wants
to get away from the telephone and the hustle and bustle. So
does Mom. Johnny, the grade-schooler, wants to go to Disney
World, since "Mike down the street is going for a *second* time
this year." And the teenage girl—well, she seems to feel just fine
in her room, talking with her friends. "The beach. Yeah. The
beach is kinda nice," she says equivocally. Or, the high school
junior, moody and blue, just grunts and gives the impression
that anything is OK, because anywhere with the family will be a
drag anyway.

Stacy Bobbs, a recent graduate from a college in Kentucky,
remembers her family vacation discussions. "My parents would
have been pained by having to go to the beach for vacation," she
says, "even though my sister and I always pushed to go there. But,
as it turns out, now I am the person who comes back paler after
Spring Break." Stacy's parents, both university professors in
Kentucky, had "higher reasons" for family vacations. Travel was
meant to broaden and was part of their children's education.

Stacy finds that her high school travels did what her parents hoped they would.

She traveled with her family, but as she grew older she also traveled with her mother and on individual trips that the family encouraged. Destinations on her travels included Kokobyu City, Japan, and places in Europe and Asia. Stacy's Japanese visit was through a Sister Cities Project.

"You are much more immersed into the culture in the Sister Cities program," she said. "I stayed with a family, and so you become part of something that you'd never even see as a regular tourist." Travel had the effect of opening her to some of her own basic assumptions, Stacy thinks. "You come back from Asia at least with a greater respect for non-Christian religions. Overall, you learn humility."

Stacy, according to the Hyatt Report's standards, would be pegged an All-American.

Of course, much family travel is to relatives' houses, so destinations are fixed for the most part. But even this kind of travel with the family opens up great opportunity. If you travel by car, you set your route and your pace, and many families trek to relatives for one leg of a more ambitious trip.

Mike Ganzenhouse gladly remembers his family vacations to his cousin's house in New Jersey. "We really looked forward to that trip every year," he recalls, "but we never really did anything except visit relatives until we got older. Then somebody realized that New York City was just a train ride away." Mike's cousins never went into the city, he says, "probably because it was right there all the time." But New York City was new to Mike, who grew up in Winston-Salem, North Carolina, and it was probably due to his itching to visit the city that his cousins woke up to its riches.

The moral? Some travel need not cover long distances, since the benefit of travel is in large part the change in perspective that comes about with the change of place. Mike's visit from afar, in one sense, allowed his cousins to have that benefit of travel without even leaving home. Travel teaches what doesn't come across in a book or in a classroom. At least that's what many parents hope. Even if it doesn't transform, travel is an opportunity to see things that are new—to do new things. And that at least broadens.

But there is a great difference between, say, being broadened by South Carolina's *South of the Border* or Florida's *Reptile Gardens* and being broadened by New York's Metropolitan Museum of Art or Washington, DC's Air and Space Museum. These are all sites, but they have different educational value. The trick is to mix Pedro's roller coaster rides with "monuments of culture and other salutary sites." You know you've created a valuable vacation when the kids take equal delight in roller coasters and monuments.

For the most part, when we delight in something, we delight in it because we know something about it. Very often, we've had a hand in creating it. The same holds true in travel, and it's especially true for teens. Delight builds on delight, and that's why successful vacations often weave current interests into the itinerary. The funny thing about discovering these interests is that parents usually need to separate their teens' interests from the prospect of travel. Ask teens to specify a place to go with their interests in mind, and what you get are destinations out of travel guides and TV commercials—not necessarily destinations really springing from genuine interests. For many (and not merely the young), travel is a special class of experience that exists apart from real life. That attitude often turns travel into escapism, and though escapism has certain merits, it usually doesn't translate into useful or educational experience.

Building on interests may be a formidable task for parents whose teens are of the Moody Blue type, and just less so for the other non-All-American profiles. For one, Moody Blues are usually not just moody and blue once they pack their luggage. They might just seem chronically in a funk. But with such teens, travel can be a good activity precisely because planning the trip is an occasion for communication. Moreover, if teens can become engaged—however slightly—in planning a trip, the trip itself gains in importance since it becomes something that they are invested in from the beginning.

So, in using teen's interests to help plan a trip, parents sometimes have to use an indirect approach. The point is to plan vacations with your teens, without succumbing to the illusion that your teens necessarily know what's best for them or even where the best destination is. Knowing a destination comes with discovery of destinations, and discovery implies striving and searching out delights.

If delight in travel uses current interests as an origin, delight in travel is intensified from learning more about destinations before anyone lugs a suitcase. Oddly enough, the first thing you might want to plan is bedtime reading. The first leg of your trip, in fact, might best have the public library as the destination.

How do interests become destinations?

Parents can identify or, to use travel metaphor, arrive at destinations by carefully discovering the places that relate to genuine interests. You can think of this as a three-step process.

First, *ask some questions about what happens at home that engages your teen's real interests*—interests that last more than a week or two. Sometimes this interest isn't simply a certain activity—say, an interest in a certain class at school, an interest in a theatrical production or other extracurricular activity, or an interest that comes up in family conversation. Sometimes it manifests itself in many related and yet distinct activities. Sometimes an interest comes out of a school project and becomes generalized—a hook that a teen hangs many experiences onto. This, of course, is usually easier to do with younger children than teens, but the principle is the same: Capitalize on enthusiasms and interests. These need not be academic—in fact, the most engaging interests for traveling teens are, more often than not, unrelated to school.

One parent says his teens had long been fascinated by volcanos. Even at a young age, the two brothers opted for National

Geographic documentaries in search of glowing eruptions and pictures of ashen skies. They had each studied the phenomena and had learned a good bit of geography in the process. This interest was a common thread in family travel.

Second, *think of events, people, places, and products that relate to the interests.* Often these spring to mind in conversation with teens. Volcanos, for example, have all sorts of interesting relationships with other things: the Hawaiian Islands, Mt. St. Helens in Washington, Mt. Pinatubo in the Philippines, Mt. Krakatoa in Indonesia, Mt. Vesuvius near Pompeii—all of these were dramatic eruptions that greatly affected history and the environment. Volcanos as geological phenomena easily make it possible to explore planetary differences—where else in the universe are there volcanos? Did you know in our solar system that there's a "volcano" of sorts that erupts nitrogen instead of magma? Or that the "seas" on the moon were formed from eruptions caused by meteorite impacts? Did you know that pumice, a rock that actually floats, is formed by volcanic eruptions—and that it is an essential ingredient in a certain rough soap called Lava? These questions help to identify related areas, and they help to broaden the particular interest into fields that admit more variety and possibility.

These pursuits are hardly trivial when they are developed broadly and woven into the curiosity of talented teens. The exploration "around" interests helps you generalize and relate experiences. What starts as a plain old volcano becomes an avenue for exploring geology, history, archeology, astronomy, even materials science (in the soap). What you are seeking at this point is general direction, not specific destinations.

Third, *retreat and consider.* If parents think about volcanos, they sometimes tend to identify the destination as Hawaii, preferably in winter, and arrange to visit a volcano or two while everyone is there. But other realities might not allow that, and in fact that vacation might not even be all that beneficial if you don't let ideas and tactics take root in interests. Take what you learn about interests and the various things that relate to them and broaden them. Then begin to consider *destinations as resources to enliven* these. Destinations are *ends* themselves for much escapist travel, but they are *means* for travel that enriches.

A caveat: If travel "broadens," it must do more than simply confirm your teen's current interests. Travel can broaden by using interests as a guide for new—and not necessarily related—interests. Design your trip so that destinations feed and deepen interests while also opening new experiences. That way, travel expands life by bringing about depth and breadth.

At this point, it's probably also reassuring to realize that virtually every destination has some educational merit—even beaches. "Our beach trips were scavenger hunts," Susan Broder recalls. "My husband, and later both boys, had salt water fish tanks. During beach trips we collected seaweeds, crabs, sea anemones, sea urchins, starfish, gorgonian corals, and surf fish for the tanks. We usually took shell identification books, too. In fact, every trip we took became a learning experience for everyone."

Of course, sometimes you just don't have anywhere to go that's, well, all that interesting. When this happens you don't necessarily have to opt for travel as escapism. Travel can become interesting by awakening interests. Begin arriving at destinations by gathering information.

You can gather information in any number of ways. You can call a travel agent and say, "We've got two weeks, *x*-number of kids, and about so-many dollars. We want to make this worthwhile for the kids, especially. Give us some ideas." The best travel agents—especially if they know you—will come up with several ideas after they ask you some additional questions about your own circumstances. Or, you can call a neighbor or a friend and say the same thing. They will also come up with several ideas. They'll probably also tell you to call so-and-so, who went to the place they themselves really wanted to go last year. There is usually no limit to opinions, but remember that one family's notion of a good time may be poison for another. And, in spite of the loads of information they have to offer, travel agents don't always know the right place for you and yours.

The point, of course, is to talk with people who travel and who know where they felt they (or their clients) have had memorable and interesting experiences. When you begin looking for information, you don't have to move quickly to decision. You go fishing for information, fully expecting to throw the small fry back along with the unpalatable species.

Sometimes, instead of looking for a place to go, a better place to start is to ask what you want to do—or what your family likes to do. Travel agents can quickly discover places that specialize in certain kinds of activities.

Publications are also good places to start, and indeed some "armchair travelers" never move from the couch to the car seat. They simply are transported by the pictures and words. Regional publications like *Southern Living* or *Midwest Living* often contain information about destinations as well as information on lodging and tourist activities. Libraries, of course, are great sources for these publications, and your travel agent will have brochures available once you have some idea about your desires. With a little library research, you can order copies of regional and travel-related periodicals.

Once you have a destination, get a map. If your family is like most, you'll choose to drive to your destination. That mode of transportation opens up still more opportunity, since you are no longer confined to *points* on maps. You can consider *lines*—infinite numbers of adjacent points—as "destinations," however instantaneous. Look for places to go through, and even stop at. Since you control direction to some extent, you can even bend the line of travel to take in points of interest. And by all means consider any point along a car trip as a possible destination.

Exploring places between the endpoint destinations becomes especially critical when you can't control the destinations—as when you go to visit relatives. But another family travel experience also puts the selection of destinations into other's hands—

in fact, your teen's hands—and that travel experience is the college tour. Admissions counselors generally agree that a campus visit is a good thing to do before teens settle on a college, and families can avoid considerable expense in special trips by folding college visits into family vacations. When it comes time to begin the process of finding a college, the interests of the college-bound teen usually take precedence. For younger siblings, that precedence need not mean that the family vacation yields all of its excitement to the elder sibling's academic plans. Despite the specific intention of the campus tours, the fact is that each campus destination racks up a good number of intervening miles; and, even for the prospective college student, forecasting the adventure of a college experience isn't just a matter of scouting out classrooms and touring libraries.

Some families minimize the hassles of discovering destinations by constantly identifying them. Building an archive of news clippings, travel-oriented magazine articles, maps, brochures, and your own recollections is quite easy—all you need is an accordion-type folder or a little niche in a file cabinet and a willingness to file items. Such archives can ease planning by putting information at your fingertips that you would otherwise be hard pressed to lay hands on, like subway maps or opening and closing times. Archives also put everything in one place, so you're less likely to find yourself searching a stack of old magazines for that article about that extraordinary place in Tennessee, or wherever.

What about preparations?

Joanna Compton, owner of Families Welcome, a travel firm in North Carolina, finds that when it comes to choosing travel destinations, two things play the leading roles: family interests and family budget. But with family travel, special needs play especially important roles, too; and special needs mean special preparation. Says Compton, "If in real estate the three keys are location, location, and location, then in family travel the three most important things are planning, planning, and planning." The more parents get the kids involved, generally the better things will go on the trip. "I suggest that families negotiate and use a principle of clustered sight-seeing," Compton says. "You go to the museums first, then hit the parks, then go to lunch." That way parents don't strain the kids too much, making it possible for them to enjoy the museums as much as the parks.

If you are comfortable with letting your teen go it alone, you should also block parts of the day to touch base and do things as a family. Schedules for teens who go off alone for an activity or independent sight-seeing provide for some level of parental control over activities. The schedule in effect limits the range of destinations and types of activities, if for no other reason than that everything takes time and some activities take place only at certain times of the day. Schedules allow you to control activities in some measure, while also allowing your teen to gain independence. Of course, agree to a means of contacting each other at all points of the day—and for that a reasonable schedule provides for predictable places and times.

Planning for a trip means getting ready to make the best use of the time—something that certainly means creating an itinerary and schedule but that also includes preparing intellectually. Again, a trip to the library might be appropriate, but don't forget about the video store, either. There are good videos to get a sneak preview of a place, and some good fiction provides a sense of a region's culture or history. If travel means going beyond the place and venturing into an experience, travelers need to provide themselves with some basic knowledge about a place before they step into it. In a sense, you need to be educated before you can use travel for education.

Stacy Bobbs remembers her trip to the Tomb of Agamemnon, also known as the Treasury of Atreus: "We went in an under-air-conditioned tour bus out to the tomb. When we got to the tomb, I was with only one or two other people to get out and look around." Troy, Helen's beauty, the treachery of Clytemnestra, and the ordeals of Electra and Orestes were not enough for the rest to venture forth. The sad thing was that the ones staying in the hot bus probably didn't know the stories.

So many places. How do we remember them?

Travel literature has a long and illustrious history, and among the standouts of its authors is Thomas Coryat, whose *Coryat's Crudities* appeared in 1608 from presses in London. The book was the product of Coryat's five-month walking tour through France, northern Italy, and Switzerland. When he got back from his trip, he hung his shoes in the village church—a less-than-literary monument to his trip—and put quill to paper.

Coryat's Crudities is a collection of his observations. "The Italians and also most strangers... in Italy do always at their meals use a little fork when they cut their meat," he observed in amazement. "This form of feeding I understand is generally used in all places in Italy." Coryat eventually ate with a fork, too, since it seemed so hygienic and sensible. He was also amazed by fans and umbrellas and "marvellous little black flat caps of felt, without any brims at all." And he labelled as "uncivil and unseemly, especially if the beholder might plainly see them," the custom among Venetian women to "walk abroad with their breasts all naked." But in addition to these sights, he committed to paper a list of the glories of Venice, enumerating and cataloging church organs, courthouses, marble statues (both "equestrial" and "pedestrial"), gondolas, and the like.

Of course, most family vacations move through places where people use forks and women wear more modest clothing than Coryat's Venetians, but new sights and "glories" still bear being put on paper. The point for teens—and for their parents—is that when you're on the road everything in a strange place is new. And it is new no matter how much reading and preparation you have done before you begin your trip. Writing about the newness is a way of identifying the kinds of differences that make travel exciting and educational. Once you train yourself to writing about the new, you begin to see the subtleties that make travel worthwhile.

In today's world, unless you travel very widely, it is easier to see likenesses than it is to see differences. This is especially the case in the United States. A McDonalds in Des Moines, Iowa isn't appreciably different from a McDonalds in San Francisco, California—or Hattiesburg, Mississippi. In fact, that McDonalds isn't that different from the one in Stuttgart, Germany!

Familiarity is reassuring and, by and large, McDonalds is a decent place to take the family for a quick meal when you're on vacation. But it isn't the kind of place that makes a vacation memorable—a fact that the moodiest of blue teens easily understands. The first trick to discovering the memorable is to write about the memorable, and write about it often. The second trick is getting the kids to do it. Here are some pointers for that second trick:

1. One person carries the writing suppplies, but everybody writes. The carrier, almost by default, is Mom or Dad—in the purse or in a pocket.
2. Whoever can't write, draws. And whoever wants to draw and write, can. Your teen's younger siblings can have a part in this, too.
3. Mom and Dad write, too.
4. Establish a schedule that everybody keeps. Let the responsibility travel from one person to the next. A good time is while waiting for dinner at the restaurant or during clean-up in the evening.
5. Everyone helps with memories, but one person writes.
6. Get everyone's commitment up front. Negotiate for it, but do not let the objective of regular writing slip.

Point six is a matter of parental art. Keep in mind that certain circumstances might not lend themselves to writing, like relative's houses. If a friend accompanies you on your family trip, that's OK. He or she can write, too. For long trips, an occasional break is acceptable, but set rules beforehand. Sometimes school

can come to your aid if you will need to take your teen out of school
for awhile. Get the school to require a log of the trip that shows
the trip's educational value. Principals and teachers are usually
very willing to help you out in this way!

But what do we write about?

Writers of travel logs know that the preservation of memories in words differs qualitatively from the memories of pho-
tographs. "We all have the certainty of our own unique way of
seeing places, a sense that the camera can be too objective a
recorder of our trips away from home," writes Thomas Mallon.
"We sometimes like the chance to say this is what I, not the Nikon,
saw. The diary still gives that."

The travel log, or "diary" as Mallon calls it, is not really
about what we saw—not, at least, primarily. The travel log pre-
serves the *experience* of what we saw, so that the Smithsonian,
say, becomes not so much a destination, a point in space, as much
as an intersection of a family's life and a famous place with its
own history and artifacts. The contours of that intersection appear
in the daily entry. To define the contours, certainly ask *what we
see*, but also explore, if only at the edges, *what it meant to us*
and *how it happened to us*.

The most interesting travel logs describe even the oddest of
experiences. For example, in 1853, Amelia Stewart Knight kept
a journal during her trip from Iowa to Oregon. Even though she
was risking her life in westward migration, she still focused on
breakfast and readying for the day's travel: "It is all hurry and
bustle to get things in order. It's children milk the cows, all hands
help yoke these cattle the devil's in them. Plutarch answers 'I
can't. I must hold the tent up, it is blowing away.' Hurrah boys.
Who tied these horses? 'Seneca, don't stand there with your hands
in your pocket. Get your saddles and be ready.'"

On the other end of the social spectrum, none other than
Queen Victoria writes about her exciting carriage accident on
October 7, 1863: "There was an awful pause, during which Alice

said: 'We are upsetting.' In another moment—during which I had time to reflect whether we should be killed or not, and thought there were still things I had not settled and wanted to do—the carriage turned over on its side, and we were all precipitated to the ground!'"

The pioneer woman prods her classically named sons and the queen "precipitates," but both used their travel logs to recall the things they saw and experienced. The truly memorable things are points when what they *saw* and what they *experienced* intertwined and commingled. That's difficult to do without some practice, but even the youngest of writers can do it.

When a fourth-grader from rural Minnesota went to Washington, DC, with his parents, part of the deal was to do a scrapbook. It was due in the teacher's hands the day school resumed for the boy, who was pulled out for this special trip. The most memorable events for him? A Washingtonian who was a fraud (not even a politician) and an impressive steam-powered tractor in the Smithsonian.

"The bus stopped and a man with a loudspeaker told us to walk by a man with a camera and pictures. He is supposed to take your picture but he doesn't really. Mom said he fools people. I got off the bus and I walked right by him. He smiled a lot and he took everybody's picture. It was kind of scary and strange." Taped to the page is a picture of the Washington Mall, the Lincoln Memorial at its focal point. On another page, in meticulously detailed pencil and crayon, stands the red tractor with a little figure of the boy standing at the base of an enormous metal wheel, perhaps made bigger by imagination and an artist's license. The boy is there "to show how big that tractor is."

Of course, getting a fourth-grader to write is sometimes easier to do than getting a teen to write. All-Americans will probably be easier to convince than Moody Blues; Hot Shots, Lone Rangers, and the Young and Restless are also tough sells. But convincing them is possible. Usually it's a matter of getting teens to invest themselves into a trip by getting their input. Once they believe that a trip may just be special, then it's easier to get them to memorialize it by writing. Stacy Bobbs kept a journal on her trips, but not on every trip she took with her family. "I only kept a journal on international trips. They were special to me, and I knew that they would be."

It's funny, but memories often emerge as products of writing itself, since sometimes the special quality of an experience isn't even discovered until pen hits the page. And then even the specialness doesn't appear until the page is read, sometimes long after the experience itself has faded.

When left to their own devices, teens have a spotty history with travel journals, because usually they paint clearer pictures of themselves as authors than of travel experiences. But even the private chronicle of teenage consciousness is better than nothing. Getting your teen to write about an experience for someone else is one of the keys, and sometimes, frankly, the family ranks pretty low as a teen's preferred readership. So, sometimes a shared family travel journal turns out to be impractical. But there are other ways to get a teen to write. Some of the most seasoned travelers find a journal odious but letters and postcards comfortable and fun. One parent says that postcard writing worked as a school assignment and as a travel journal when her daughter was asked by a language teacher to send postcards to her so that she could share them in class.

But, if it can be done, do the family round-robin journal. As a matter of fact, do it without your teen's help, if you must. Your teen might see the light mid-way on the trip.

How do we keep the journal from becoming an itinerary?

Questions usually help fill out what could become an itinerary of destinations in a family travel log. "Today, we did the art museum, the science show, and played in a park. We saw a statue," some are tempted to write. But so what? *So what?*—those are the essential words, though for writers to write better they need better guidance than an incriminating "So what?" Here are some ways to move from the grocery list to a real travel log:

1. To begin with, ask what was memorable. What did we see, what did we do today that seems worth noting? Sometimes this is the unexpected—the fake photographer in Washington, the bell-hop in the hotel, the television personality, the homeless person. Sometimes it's meeting with a place of considerable history—the steps of the Lincoln Memorial, the Empire State Building, Independence Hall, the Vatican.

2. Describe what happened when we saw it or when we did it.

3. Who else was there? Was this a normal situation for the place, or were there "special circumstances"?

4. What details come to mind that seem to make this memorable? Focus on the experience in terms of how it unfolded—that is, in terms of its process. A statue has "details," but what's really important is the way that the statue's attributes impress themselves onto our experience.

5. If someone were looking at us while we were experiencing this memorable whatever, what would we have looked like?

6. Does everybody feel the same way about this event? If not, why? Is this experience something that only we know about, or is it something everybody experiences?

7. What did we need to know beforehand in order to have this experience?

8. How did this experience change our perspective on things? Did this make things less or more confusing?

9. What kind of new questions do we have?

Remember that memories are not always enjoyable and that some things happen like thunderbolts and roller coasters, rolling upon us without much mercy or concern. If travel "broadens," it opens new possibilities, new ambiguities, and new questions—the kinds of outcomes that escapist travel never really offers, but even escapist destinations can yield.

What to Do About Work

Are teens who hold after-school jobs making a good investment in themselves?

Forget what you know about teens and working, if for no other reason than there is no right answer. Just when you put down the article on the detrimental effects employment during high school has on teens, your neighbor hangs her head over the fence with news about her son, Bobby, and how he's a National Merit Scholar, placed first in this year's state science contest, is playing two sports, writes for the school newspaper, and works thirty hours a week before school assembling atmospheric testing equipment. Who can figure?

To make matters worse, there's a confusing array of statistics that allude to distinctions between bright kids who work and average kids who work—as if statistics tell the complete story, which, of course, they can't.

Still, you satisfy yourself that your teen won't want to work. "*My* Tommy," you think, "he won't even pick up his clothes. How's he going to hold a job?" But you're wrong about this, because, if your teen is like most teens, work will come up. And you, once again, have to make the call.

Confusing though high school employment may seem, it helps to arm yourself with answers and anecdotes about teenage employment.* Know how to guide your teen because employment, especially in the mid-teenage years, has the potential to monkey a great deal with your teen's life—for better or worse. All kids are different, and the only thing of which you can be certain is that your teen's employment opportunity, that terrific job your teen is dying to take that just happens to be during the school year, will be unique.

Does working build character?

We hear a lot of talk about a "work ethic"—usually in reference to someone who doesn't have one. Parents, for the most part, don't want their teen lying around the house, and, in fact, if you ask your friends or co-workers whether they would encourage their teenagers to work, you'll most likely find an overwhelmingly affirmative response. Work is good—you've no doubt heard it said many times before. Achievement, we know, goes hand-in-hand with effort, but before you send your teen off to an after-school job, make sure you're clear about what *you* think your teen can achieve. If it's better grades, a more rounded lifestyle, or simply to develop a "work ethic" at an early age, you may be overestimating what a job at the local hardware store can really provide. Statistics bear this out. Anecdotes, on the other hand, don't.

Take one recent graduate of the master of accounting program at the University of North Carolina at Chapel Hill. This

---

*Teenage employment issues in this chapter always refer to employment during the school year, unless noted otherwise.

fellow began working as a high school freshman busing tables and freely admits he did it "for the money." Even with a few years of maturity under his belt, this grad looks back on high school employment as a positive experience and remembers his parents as being highly encouraging. "Working made me try harder, and even though it limited some extracurricular things, I learned to budget my time and my money. I enjoyed being somewhat independent from my parents." And he says it didn't affect his grades at all.

The experts might counter those kinds of claims. Even though work is *supposed* to make teenagers learn responsibility and better understand the value of money, the fact is, most of what they earn is spent on themselves, without regard to future needs. Anne Bailey, assistant professor in the department of family and consumer sciences at Miami University of Ohio, writes, "Working teenagers may develop attitudes of possessiveness toward free

"THINGS JUST HAVE'NT BEEN THE SAME IN MY STORE SINCE I HIRED THAT KID RALPH."

time and the income they earn. When these young people leave home and find they must pay for all household expenses and assume responsibility for household tasks, they very likely experience a drop in their level of living and increased constraints on their leisure time." But who doesn't?

Ask most teens and you'll find a positive impression of working. In one survey, three-fourths of teenagers questioned said working had a positive impact on their lives. And most parents would agree.

What do teens do with their money?

The short answer is that they waste it—some $60 billion a year on themselves. Through jobs, allowance, and gifts from parents, teens nationwide have around $60 to spend each week on anything they choose. As a parent working to support a household, there may be few weeks when you have $60 to spend any way you please. But kids are different, and they are buying everything from cars to make-up to long-distance service.

Many teens are making much more money, however, depending on how much they work and what they do—often upwards of $200 a week. And their numbers are growing: Nearly forty percent of teens sixteen and seventeen years of age are working as cashiers, salespeople, cooks, waiters, stock movers, receptionists, and the like. The more enterprising teens, and the ones more academically able, often find themselves doing work well beyond their years—like programming and accounting. One teen says that his computer skills and basic knowledge in accounting led to a key position in a small business. "I was their accounting department. I was making three times what my friends were making."

With this money, teens have turned into a very significant segment of the consumer market. They want cars, Reeboks® that pump, expensive clothes, and electronics. One survey showed that nearly half of all teens own a TV, more than the number who own a phone. Says the teenage accountant, "I had a great car—a convertible—plus money to spend on nearly anything I wanted. I was making more money than my mother."

Actually, though, kids do save, too—at a pace that's about as high as their parents, some 4.5% of earnings. Parents make the case that with food, housing, transportation, and everything else costing what it does, there's little room to save. Your teen, though, might make the same case. Many of their expenses are deemed "necessities," and your help is certainly needed to sort through what's really important.

With the lure of work and money, teenagers are working more and more. Child-labor violations are skyrocketing, and parents seldom know what the legal limits are. In North Carolina, for example, teens have strict numbers of hours and times of the day they are allowed to work, depending on their age and whether school is in or out of session. So compelling is the desire of teens to work that the state recently adopted new laws to prevent teens from working after 11:00 p.m. Teachers and educators complained that many students were so worn out at the beginning of the school day that they could not perform in class. Also, teens in North Carolina under eighteen are not allowed to do hazardous work or certain kinds of work in establishments selling alcohol. These state laws are administered by work permits, required for anyone under eighteen seeking employment. Most states have some type of work permit requirement which requires both parent and employer signatures. Some states even allow schools to administer work permit programs to prevent students who perform poorly in school from working.

However, most state work permit coordinators recognize that many children are working without a legal right to do so. And they also know that the programs aren't panaceas for ensuring your teen is safe in a work environment. Employers often don't know state rules on employment or fudge them in desperation to fill work schedules and positions. One large southeastern food chain is battling literally hundreds of child labor violations from infractions as minor as exceeding the three-hour-per-day maximum for teens fifteen and under, to employing teens around dangerous meat-cutting equipment.

Teenage employment kills hundreds and injures thousands
more each year. Even innocuous-sounding jobs often have an
element of danger: the hot grease fryer in the local restaurant or
the cardboard crusher in your corner market. And farm jobs are
the most deadly of all—a place where upwards of two million
children work without benefit of state or federal child labor regulations, or the watchful eye of the Occupational Safety and
Health Administration. Again, you as a parent have a responsibility to know what your teen will be doing on the job. What this
means for you if you let your teen work: Keep up with your teen's
schedule and know the kind of work your teen performs.

Which teens work?

Kids in general want to work, and even in recent years when
the economy has been less than peachy, teens respond positively about their ability to achieve success by working hard and
educating themselves. Few teens today, though, are working for
the family as a whole, a dramatic change from when you or your
parents were growing up. Children are working for social and
psychological reasons rather than family economic ones. Parents,
too, make few demands on teens as to how they spend their
money. Fewer than one-fourth of parents insist that teens set
aside money for college. Only three percent of parents say they
ask children to help out with day-to-day family expenses.

When you look at who is working among teens, you find
them in families which are more affluent and have better educated
parents. Perhaps the desire to work in teens is based on parental
role models, or perhaps affluence provides a greater edge in finding a job, but in either case, because we know that parents of
academically talented children are better educated and more
affluent, it's easy to imagine that more of these kids are going to
be working.

Youth apprenticeships are on the rise, especially with a presidential mandate to support programs which help kids make the transition from high school to workplace. Most of the kids served by apprenticeships are not college-bound. Often, though, these apprenticeships do couple additional education beyond the high school years with work. While four-year colleges don't figure prominently into these programs yet, it is easy to imagine that they will in the near future. In fact, certain types of graduate programs like business and clinical psychology are becoming increasingly insistent that candidates have relevant work experience.

However, high school work may not be particularly relevant on a college application. John Anderson, dean of admissions at Kenyon College, says that when they see an applicant whose grades are not up to par and who worked a great deal in high school, the work experience often reflects negatively. By the same token, if an applicant needs financial aid and hasn't worked, that, too, may be treated negatively. Jennifer Trussell, director of admissions at Mississippi College, adds that admissions committees would rather see students spending time with school, but if an applicant does work, it may be important to understand how he or she spent the money.

Still, you'll likely find your teen thinks he or she can successfully balance not only school and work, but extracurriculars and community involvement as well. Often they can, but just as often they can't. For parents willing to take that risk, here are some of the findings researchers have discovered about teens who work:

In a national study of teenagers working during the tenth, eleventh, and twelfth grades, total hours worked during high school negatively affected seventeen of twenty-two possible outcomes, even after researchers adjusted the data for socio-economic variables. Outcomes that were affected adversely by the number of hours worked included going to college, high school attendance, standardized test scores, academic self-concept, and behavior. This last aspect is particularly disturbing because it was found that employment in high school may tend to promote rather than deter delinquent behavior and increase alcohol and drug use. Contrary to what many would expect, the researchers found that, for many teens, high school employment actually fosters negative attitudes toward work itself.

But the issue might not be just work. Teens working in college actually do better academically, and many teens in high school handle work just fine. It's evident that other teens working in high school don't handle the responsibility nearly as well. Maturity may be one reason why, but other factors should be considered as well. For one, high school employment is often in low-skill, boring jobs that for many teens seem not to relate to much of anything. Their sole benefit may be the paycheck, and even at their young age, teens already voice heavy preference for making less money in a job that's enjoyable.

Another important factor in a teen's ability to manage school and a job may be his or her reasons for working. Those with clear, long-term financial goals in mind seem to do better than others. For example, teens who worked to save money for college had many more positive outcomes in the study mentioned above. Perhaps the most important positive outcome, however, was whether they actually attended college, with those saving toward that goal much more likely to attend. All of this makes sense when applied to teens working in college. With the clear purpose of paying for one's education in mind, the chance to focus, manage time wisely, and do well is enhanced.

The key to employment during high school, like everything else, may be moderation. In almost every study available on high school employment, the number of hours worked is the only variable closely related to positive and negative outcomes. In fact, it may be the amount of time detracted from school, not the time dedicated to work itself, that is the culprit for these negative aspects. When school is not a factor, all rules change. Writes Herbert Marsh in *Sociology of Education*, "In contrast to working during the school year, working during the summer appears to have some benefits and no apparent costs."

How much is too much? Everyone's different, but the dividing line between acceptable and too much seems to be twenty hours per week during the school year. Still, for many, that will seem to be a lot. The Child Labor Coalition, a group trying to strengthen child labor laws, proposes the twenty-hour limit for sixteen- and seventeen-year-old employees when school is in session. In fact, some states have already adopted rules that meet or exceed that expectation, and more states are likely to follow.

Do you draw a line in the sand?

With three out of four high school seniors working, the likelihood is great that you will face the work issue with your teen during high school. And you may believe that work does provide many positive benefits and that your teen can handle the responsibility. Still, it's best to lay down some rules.

First, teens seem to do better with goals. You should consider guidelines on what your teen can and cannot do with their earnings: how much is saved, how much is spent on personal items, how much is discretionary. Be careful, too, to help your teen avoid debt and significant financial obligations. Many parents, for instance, co-sign car loans or expect teens to meet repair and insurance responsibilities for cars. These can become financial obligations that literally force teens to work even during those times when they know it would be better if they cut back or passed altogether on employment. Now may also be a good time to explore college financing options, too, and if your teen is expected to pay part of the college costs, that can be a goal worth working toward.

Second, define the type of work that is acceptable. Some parents believe it's good to have their teens find jobs on their own, but if a phone call from you could help them land a more interesting, better-paying job, consider doing it. If you don't want your teen working in a grocery store, construction, or some other job, you can bet they'll want an alternative. It might be comforting to know that no link has been found between first jobs and future occupational outcomes, so flipping burgers at the local hamburger hut does not mean that your teenage math scholar won't find his or her way into a high-paying electrical engineering career. Still, if you do want to see your child doing something relevant, consider volunteer work. One teen says to improve his chances for acceptance into a veterinary program, he gave his time to a university's primate center. Other than not being paid, everything else about the job proved positive, including a couple of impressive recommendations.

Third, remember that the amount of work you allow your teen to engage in is crucial, particularly for younger teens. Unless there is a pressing need for money, work should be treated as "something extra" and not as a priority, even if setting money aside for college is important. Better grades may well create more college resources in terms of scholarships and grants than three high school years of saving for college.

Finally, treat work as a reward for your teen doing well with his or her real job: school. And remember that school is an education about many things, some of which are found in after-school clubs, sports, and hangout time with friends. If your teen can't lead a full life, perhaps work should be the first item cut, not the last.

If you can swing it, the best of all possible worlds may be to limit your teen's work to summer employment. He or she will get all the benefits with few drawbacks, and it would be something you can most likely encourage heartily without worrying about detrimental effects.

Can your teen pass Collegiate Employment 101?

As the parent of an academically talented teen, your interest is likely not in preparing your teen for the workforce, but rather for college. But here's the kicker: With college costs being what they are, a lot of teens will need and are expected to work in college to meet soaring tuition costs. So important is your teen's college work effort that employment and work-study programs on college campuses are an integral part of financial aid

Looking Back on Teenage Employment

My first job was one summer in one of those sprawling super-markets of the late sixties. It anchored a strip shopping center, long before malls became the rage. I was sixteen, earning $1.60 an hour, the minimum wage. What I learned then, but did not realize until much later in life, was that each work experience was a building block and that at some point in life, all those blocks make something, in my case a career that I enjoy, that I make a very good living at.

Every job teaches something, and this first supermarket job taught me much. I learned to serve others, to bag their groceries and put them in their cars—no tipping allowed. I learned to be nice to everyone, that the customer was always right. I learned something about marketing, about how people would swamp the store—even get ugly—for specials like four loaves of bread for a dollar, or two half gallons of ice cream for 99¢, or five pounds of ground beef for $4.99. I still remember those prices twenty-five years later.

I learned about the nature of employees, how a line seemed to separate those bent on cheating and those who learned better from their parents. Some employees stole food, serious food like steaks and hams and the gourmet stuff, but they didn't call what they did stealing. They somehow felt they were entitled to whatever was in the store. Every employee cheated by waiting for the quarter hour, the process of standing around an extra eight minutes so one could be paid for a full extra fifteen minutes. We were informally trained on how to do it, and I did it. I never questioned the rightness or wrongness of it until years later when my subordinates stood around on me.

That first job brought to life values taught by my mother and father that had never before been tested. They seemed to be tested nightly as the stockers and baggers hung out in the parking lot after work shooting the bull. It was there that I decided that I would never

Continued on page 117.

packages and generally have paid administrators. Here's how it works:

Your son or daughter applies to, let's say, an Ivy League school and is accepted. The total cost is $22,000 per year, not at all unusual. You, having done well in life, have a household income of say $75,000 before taxes, or about $50,000 after taxes. You own the better part of your home, a couple of cars, have saved a bit for retirement, and are seemingly well off financially—before you pay out college costs. Doing so leaves you just $28,000 on which to live, and, as you know, it doesn't go far. But chances are your teen won't qualify for any kind of financial aid because you own and earn too much, so one alternative is for teens to work during college to help pay the cost.

Some colleges, strapped for money, consider the need for financial aid in their decision on whether to accept certain students. (But don't encourage your teenager to hide financial need on the application. If they can't afford to attend, being accepted won't matter. Besides, colleges tell you up front what their policies are regarding financial aid.) Many colleges offer to cover one hundred percent of your demonstrated need. Demonstrating need, however, is the tough part, but maybe your teen does qualify for financial aid. What they get is basically a "package" that includes grants, loans, scholarships, some of your money, and, you guessed it, employment for your teen. And if college-bound Bobby decides he can't work and go to college at the same time, well, he'll forfeit that part of his financial aid package and you will have to make up the difference.

One reason colleges are so insistent on students working is that, statistically, students who work do slightly better academically in college than students who don't work. Most colleges won't actually come out and brag about this, but the bottom line is that the differences in grade point averages between working students and non-working students is so small, they are convinced that working has no negative effects. In fact, three hundred graduating college seniors in one study said work was an opportunity for a smoke cigarettes, and I never did. I also decided that I could be one of the guys and have a beer, in moderation, and my value about drinking has remained virtually unchanged over the years (although I'm the first to admit now that I was too young to drink, but that was 1969).

I could have become a thief working at the supermarket. I could have been a drunk driver. I could have lost my interest in education and merely strived for that time when I would be earning $4.00 an hour. A lot of the "friends" I made that summer did. But the combination of the positive value system of my parents and the work experience in the supermarket allowed me to learn something that parents alone, or a supermarket alone, could not have taught me.

Throughout my teenage years and early twenties, I held many jobs. I returned to the supermarket two years later to wrap produce. I also counseled at a summer camp, pumped gas (a dying art), and worked in a sheet metal fabrication plant. I worked construction one summer and worked in a research lab—all for pay. So much did I want to work in the hyperbaric chamber at Duke University Medical Center that I worked there for two months as a volunteer. Ironically, I would come back three years later, not as an employee but as a patient, needing decompression from a diving accident. It was a nice time to know people.

Working teaches much. Perhaps no parent would argue the point, but often in an effort to give our children the best, we overlook what is best for them. Had I been a parent and known all about the supermarket, I may not have wanted my son working there. I would be afraid for him, that he would become a thief or a drunk or a dropout. Not that I'm a bad parent, or that he's a bad child, but fear changes how you act. But that decision would not be the best one. He should be allowed to work.

Like everything, however, employment during high school needs to be taken for what it is and what it is not. It's not the big step in life, it doesn't replace school, and it won't necessarily make you a better person.

—*Webb Howell*

new kind of social life, gave them a feeling of fulfillment, helped them attain new skills, and improved their self image. They also reported on some of the negative aspects, but those were not unlike any that one would find in a work-related situation. Studies that focus on freshmen alone find similar results and even support the claim that college jobs provide greater discipline and structure for freshmen who suddenly find themselves more independent than ever before.

There is a correlation between the student's academic ability and his or her ability to manage both school and work. Students with higher college admission test scores, by far, were able to handle employment in college better than their less academically able counterparts, by virtue of their grade point average. Even academically able students who worked twice the number of hours as others earned as high or higher GPAs by the end of their freshman year.

One should hasten to add that the virtues of work are often measured in test scores, and if students are making good grades, they are assumed to be happy and well-adjusted. On the college level, there is little research that refutes this notion, but as parents we must remind ourselves that it's our kid out there, far away from home, hitting the books, and working twenty to thirty hours a week, and not some researcher's statistic.

What prepares teens for the future?

How many times have you heard, "How can I get a job if no one will give me a chance to gain some experience?" Your teen will likely use that one on you to convince you that a job today means employment experience for the future. However, the likelihood is that employers in your teen's future won't care whether an applicant worked at Bob's Quickie Mart. The jobs are likely to be so disparate in skills that the teenage work experience is probably moot.

Employers do want skills. The US Department of Education's publication, *What Works*, says business leaders look for students with solid basic skills and positive work attitudes. New technology means that abilities in writing, mathematics, reasoning, and problem solving—skills best developed in the classroom—are the most important factors in gaining employment. Other skills like self-discipline, reliability, perseverance, teamwork, accepting responsibilities, and respect for others can be taught in high school employment opportunities, but they also can be developed in many other high school activities just as well. And perhaps too often, high school jobs don't develop these kinds of qualities and absorb too much time for them to be learned elsewhere.

Diverse skills learned in the classroom are also going to be important in the emerging job market of the future. Whereas your parents likely held a job or career for a lifetime, workers of tomorrow will have to be more diverse. The ability to change and to adapt to work assignments is developed in high school and college. As one grows, however, work becomes a key learning ground. But the question about high school employment is a matter of time and priorities. Can your teen get more from school and its associated activities or from a job at the corner market? In college, the question might be "Can I, as a student, get more from a fraternity social or from helping a world-class professor edit a manuscript?" Granted, many campus jobs aren't that glamorous, but the point is that, eventually, the opportunity to make work a significant learning experience comes into play. For many, though, high school employment doesn't fill this bill.

It may be tough for parents to admit that sometimes work may not be a good thing to do. It is counter to our upbringing and our conditioning as parents. But, like everything else about parenting, the issues are never simple, and for your teen to get the most out of his or her high school years, everything—even the job at the corner market—must be considered carefully.

What to Do About Getting Into College

And why some bright students don't make the grade.

Terry Bennett had set his sights on Stanford in the seventh grade. His room had a Stanford pennant, he wore a Stanford baseball cap, and he lived in his Stanford sweatshirt. It was all he wanted in a college, and he knew Stanford just had to admit him. He had top grades and was captain of the soccer team. Most important was that he loved Stanford University and knew it was the only place for him. Terry couldn't wait to apply and get his acceptance—so he was crushed when he didn't get in.

Unexpected? Definitely. Unfair? Maybe. But it's a scenario more common than you think, and though you can't always avoid it, you and your teen can be more prepared if you see the college admissions process in the proper light. It may be helpful to recognize at the outset that the college selection process is not an equation that you can solve, not a mystery you can unravel. Rest a little easier in the knowledge that oversights in the selection process are rare. They are kept to a minimum because admission officers are professionals who are familiar with most secondary schools in the country; who interact constantly with college counselors; who pay very close attention to the nuances in applications; and who discuss and debate applicants' merits prior to reaching decisions. Their charge is to identify and enroll the very best class possible.

It's also helpful to know, in broadest terms, what admissions committees consider when they begin reviewing applications. Essentially, they focus on what an applicant has done for the past four or five years. The evaluation covers a range of areas, and individual colleges stress different points. There are, however, three areas of critical importance which you can be sure are part of the evaluation: academic accomplishment in terms of grades, class rank, and courses taken; standardized test scores; and character, which is reflected by extracurricular activities and recommendations.

Still, college admissions is more than the ideal rank+scores+activities candidate. Lots of students, just like Terry Bennett, come close to the ideal, but they don't get in. What gives?

Why wouldn't my teen be accepted?

Maybe the most harmful way your teen can approach the college search is with the I-can-go-to-any-college-I-choose attitude. "If you don't think any place is above you," says one academically talented student who has just been through the process, "step back and get humble." Help your teen keep a firm grip on reality—in particular, your teen needs to understand what a particular college is looking for when it chooses students. This understanding helps you get around the pressures and disappointments that occur when a student concentrates on colleges where admission may be out of reach, for one reason or another.

One reason why even the brightest students are sometimes denied admission to competitive colleges is that the definition of a "great student" varies from college to college. Take, for instance, the case of one high school, whose valedictorian, National Merit semi-finalist, nominee in the Westinghouse Science Talent Search, and straight-A student council president were all denied admission to their top-choice colleges. Why?

Well, the Westinghouse entrant was denied because there were twenty other Westinghouse entrants, including the national winner, in the applicant pool. Also in the pool were several Bausch and Lomb Award winners along with a handful of people who had pursued special science research projects at colleges and national laboratories during the summer. Still, the applicant in question was a fine candidate. Had the college's applications not jumped unexpectedly by fifteen percent when they were projected to drop, she might have been admitted. As it was, though, the competition was grueling and some fine distinctions had to be drawn.

The valedictorian's rank lost its clout when her reviewers discovered that all she did was hit the books year after year. She cared only about producing high grades. Her recommendations were dull because there was little to say about her. There was no evidence to suggest that she would make any substantial contributions in or out of the classroom.

The National Merit semi-finalist—whose case testifies to the fact that high standardized test scores alone don't guarantee college admission—had phenomenal scores across the board. He fell into the group of students that one admissions officer refers to as "those who have the power and talent but whose achievement is not commensurate." This student's grades were not weak, but it was clear from his course selection and recommendations that he was capable of far more scholarship than he had produced. He was neither testing his limits nor taking advantage of the curriculum.

The student council president falls into the category of the "last-minute-shoot-yourself-in-the-foot" candidate. These students know they're bright and have everything in line, so rather than presenting themselves in a powerful, persuasive way on the application, they exhibit a cocky attitude. One admissions officer notes that students like this seem to be asking, "Why do I have to turn myself inside out?" That doesn't make a lot of points in many admissions offices.

But the various definitions of "a great student" aren't the only thing that makes admissions unpredictable. There's also the concept of student body diversity. When a college builds a freshman class, it wants to create a community of bright students who represent many different sectors. This collection of people, representing different ideas and experiences, makes for a truly stimulating intellectual and social environment.

Diversity itself is defined in many ways but includes social, ethnic and economic background, as well as the range of academic and extracurricular experiences a student has had. Since students learn as much from each other as they do in the classroom, a truly diverse student body relates as much to the quality of the education as do teaching and physical resources. Diversity works like this: Suppose your family lives in a rural area, and your teen applies to a competitive college where there are few "rural" students. Assuming your teen is academically well-prepared, the geographic factor may be just the boost he or she needs to be admitted. On the flip side, of course, there is an equally well-prepared student, from a metropolitan area which is over-represented at that college, who may not be admitted. Encourage your teen to demonstrate any diversity he or she can bring to the student body—anything that sets him or her apart from the crowd—on the application.

Always remember that college admissions relies heavily on human judgment, namely the judgment of the admissions committee. In the decision process, hope for the best but prepare realistically for every possibility. Teens need to understand that rejection doesn't mean that they can't do the work—it's just a matter of what are a college's particular needs. When it comes to college admissions, teens should try to develop a realistic outlook that neither deters them from striving toward their goals nor crushes them if their goals are not attained.

What do colleges want?

That's all the bad news—your teen may not get in at at the college of his or her choice. But there's plenty your teen can do to be ready for the intense competition. First and foremost is academic preparation. All colleges are concerned with a student's preparation in the traditional areas of English, natural science, math, foreign language, and social science. To get a sense of what an applicant has achieved in these areas, admissions committees assess the applicant's high school profile, which indicates the level of courses available at the applicant's high school. The more competitive colleges expect an applicant to have taken the most rigorous courses available and to have maintained a full academic load during high school.

The applicant pool of a selective college includes students from all sorts of high schools, both public and private. Many of these schools offer an incredible array of honors and advanced courses, while others may have a comparatively weak curriculum. The key is that your teen take the best courses the school has to offer. If yours is a relatively weak school system, enrolling in math, language, or science courses at a local college may help your teen prepare for a competitive college. Not only will he or she advance academically, but admissions committees will likely be impressed. Admissions committees consider how their applicants sought challenge—in their own school and elsewhere—during high school.

Start early! If your teen is to take the most challenging courses possible, you must plan ahead. When your teen is in middle school, think about what advanced courses he or she should be taking in the junior or senior year of high school, when the college search is in full swing. Then, with that framework in mind, think one year ahead and figure out which courses will put your teen in the position he or she wants to be in four or five years down the road. For example, if your teen is in the seventh grade and wants to take calculus in high school, then he or she needs to get ready for an advanced math sequence. In terms of planning one year ahead, he or she probably needs to take algebra I in the eighth grade.

How do you know what advanced courses your teen will want to take in four or five years? Chances are your high school has a college prep track that more or less dictates what your teen will take, with some options here and there. Nonetheless, always encourage your teen to aim high and take the best possible courses—with a broad variety. Find out what prerequisites are necessary for any advanced courses, so your teen will be prepared. Planning ahead and choosing the best courses may be obvious advice, but doing both these things will allow your teen more options later on.

But remember that academics are not everything. There are about sixteen thousand high schools in the US, and they're full of students who take challenging courses. Since applicant pools at selective colleges are overflowing with bright students, extracurricular involvement plays an important role in college admissions. And since colleges do care about more than good grades, there ought to be a balance between what your teen needs to study to prepare for college and what your teen finds interesting outside the classroom. If your teen is interested in, say, music or art, you should lend a hand in time management and help him or her find the time and ways to pursue those interests. Activities are more than padding for a college application. High school is a time for your teen to build self-confidence and to discover and develop talent. Extracurricular activities are just the ticket.

In terms of college admissions, there are no right or wrong activities. Indeed, the high school years are a time for your teen to experiment and think about possibilities and aspirations. Give your teen the freedom to try many things but also encourage him or her to find an activity for which he or she has genuine passion. Genuine passion is important to admissions committees, and it tends to be evident in an application because students get deeply involved and make a difference in their club or organization. Admissions committees easily spot "clubbers"—students who have many superficial involvements but no depth or evidence of real commitment. An admissions committee doesn't care so much about how many or what activities an applicant participates in as it does about a deep commitment to some cause or organization.

Extracurricular involvements also give your teen the chance to form relationships with teachers and other adults—relationships that provide important developmental and practical benefits. It's never too early for a mentor, and often a good teacher can recognize talent in your teen and help advise and direct his or her involvement in a club or organization. That person may also become important as someone who can provide an in-depth personal recommendation for college admission.

What's involved in the actual college search?

Each spring, admissions officers visit hundreds of secondary schools, conduct city-wide receptions, and attend college fairs. Back on their home campuses they interview, write to, and telephone thousands of young people and greet scores of parents. In early winter they begin evaluating mountains of applications containing reams of paper. They log untold (and unpaid) hours of overtime, and accumulate strings of seven-day work weeks. All this they do under the constant pressure of deadlines, first to finish evaluations, then to make selections, and finally to produce and mail decision letters. The process is educational, challenging, and, at times, exhausting. They feel a sense of accomplishment, but they cannot relax. The intensity of the process will not subside until the next class is in place. And that will occur not next week but many months hence.

And while admissions officers are doing their part to put together a class, your teen should take advantage of every opportunity to learn about various colleges. College fairs at the high school are an excellent way to begin, and even in ninth grade your teen can get some valuable insight from walking through a college fair. Younger students may not get the attention of a junior or senior, but they will certainly learn much by listening. Most college representatives are happy to share information with younger students who are trying to understand and prepare for the college admissions process.

In the early stages of the college search, it's important to keep options open. In other words, look past the name value of a college, for the "name" college is a dangerous concept indeed. Everything in our culture, including most people, tells students to go to the biggest college they can get in, whether it is a name based on athletic or academic reputation. Think about the college search as you would the search for a new jacket. A Giorgio Armani coat is a fine coat with a well-respected name. The way they are made, though, they only fit well and look good on certain people. Five-foot, 235-pound men do not look good in Armani coats. The person who buys a coat considering only the name, and not the qualities, is bound to look silly and be unhappy with the choice.

Don't encourage your teen to go to a college because it is prestigious, and encourage your teen not to shun a college because its name is not prestigious. There are lots of campus settings, any one of which may be right for your teen and all of which your teen should probably at least consider at the outset. Among the possibilities are the small liberal arts college, the large state university, the mid-sized university, the large private university, the technical college, and the single-sex college. Encourage your teen to look at these schools for what qualities they offer, not what the name offers.

By the junior year of high school, your teen should be searching earnestly for the right college. Get one or two college guidebooks like Barron's, Fiske, *The College Guide for Academically Talented Students*, or others. These guides are a good source of statistics on school size, majors, annual volume of applications, and the percentage of applicants admitted. Some of the books also go into depth with background information regarding residential life. Your teen should also actively explore colleges by doing things like attending school-sponsored receptions in your area, initiating discussions with the high school's college counselor, and meeting with college admissions representatives who may visit your teen's school. Your teen should also be getting on college mailing lists. Students who have already taken standardized tests and done well or who belong to certain organizations may be placed on some lists automatically, but your teen can also request to be put on a particular college's mailing list. Your teen's first goal in all these preparations, of course, is to decide which colleges are interesting, and each of these sources provides an additional piece to the puzzle.

What should my teen look for in a school?

Chances are, once your teen really starts looking at colleges, he or she will find a fair number of them interesting. In order to whittle that long list into a short list, your teen needs to investigate each college. Some things to consider include the quality of the faculty, academic programs, and student life. Your teen should also consider his or her personal preferences as to size and location. Don't let your teen forget to consider how happy and successful he or she might be as a student at a particular college. Look closely at the academic and personal advising systems: How do students choose a major? Who does the advising? How accessible are faculty? There are real differences here among the very best schools, so seek answers that seem to provide the best fit for your teen.

To a certain extent, your teen can get answers to these questions by reading and talking to the admissions office (which you should always treat as a resource). But in order to get a real understanding of a college, your teen needs to go beyond books and the admissions office and connect with students and faculty. This is where the legendary "campus visit" comes into play. Visiting is the most expensive part of the college search, but it's also the most important part of the whole process. Ideally, you and your teen will visit campuses late in the junior year or very early in the senior year. Summer is usually an easy time for families to travel, but be warned: College campuses have a completely different feel when the students are gone for the summer. Unless it's absolutely impossible, visit while classes are in session.

Take every advantage of your time on campus. Be nosy and wander through classroom buildings and the library. Sit in on a class. Strike up conversations with random students. Eat in a dining hall. Be sure to give your teen some room to move, and let him or her be a college student for a day. The thrill of visiting a college campus, however, may distract your teen a bit from what's important about a college, so help your teen keep his or her feet planted on the ground. All the campus tours in the world won't tell you a thing about what a college has to offer. Georgian architecture and big trees, nice as they are, do not a college make.

In addition to discovering the academic and social aspects of a college, ask questions about graduation and retention rates. All colleges will lose some students, but if it seems too many are leaving, there may be a serious problem. Find out when students are leaving and why. Pick up as many issues of the school newspaper as you can—even subscribe to it—since the newspaper is a wonderful gauge of campus life and issues. It's inherent to the life of a university for the relationship between students and the administration to be tense, but there should at least be a healthy dialogue. You may read about frustration because students can't get the classes they want, dissatisfaction with faculty accessibility, racial tension, or students transferring because of financial difficulties. These are real problems that can affect a student's happiness. As you explore campus issues, distinguish between these issues and the natural tensions that crop up on campuses.

What can I do to help my teen succeed in college?

Assuming good planning, your teen will end up with acceptances come April and will be ready to commence a new stage in life. Of course, once your teen goes off to college, he or she will begin to experience new freedoms. These new freedoms mean some level of independence from you, and that means plenty of decisions to make. Decisions in college, like decisions in the real world, come in all shapes and sizes. College students decide on a daily basis whether they'll go to class, how much time they'll spend studying, and whether they'll eat a healthy meal. They also make decisions about alcohol, sex, money, and more. You, as a parent, will no doubt worry that your teen will make mistakes and, of course, your teen will.

Yes, there are things that can go wrong in college. Some students simply don't live up to expectations gradewise. Some spend money foolishly. Some may get themselves in academic trouble and refuse to get help. Some will simply experiment with a new lifestyle that's not particularly conducive to doing well in college. But even those students who start college on the wrong foot usually get through okay. How? They know—or learn—how to make good decisions.

The high school years, in general, are a time to allow your teen to learn to make decisions while he or she is still in your care. And while parents may not be able to hold their teen's hand in college, they can get them ready to go it alone. The experience of making decisions is a big part of a teenager's development. When your teen is searching for a college, let him or her make the decisions. Give your teen some input, but don't run the show. It's your teen's search, and colleges want to hear from students, not parents.

Feeling the Heat

If teens have so few responsibilities, why do they feel so much pressure?

Six weeks into her junior year of high school, Amy Martin surprised her parents and herself by throwing a sixteen-year-old's version of a temper tantrum. When her parents protested her decision to drop out of her school's art club, Amy simply began to scream. Her screams then became uncontrollable tears. "Even though I'm really into art and had been in the club since freshman year," Amy says now, "I didn't have enough time for it this year, with all the other meetings, rehearsals, and practices I was supposed to be at." Plus, she knew that the club's weekend outings to museums and exhibitions would interfere with her family's plans to visit college campuses. "My parents couldn't understand why I had to

quit—they thought I should stick with this activity I had started," she says. But, instead of being able to explain her decision
to them rationally, she exploded with worries that she now real-
izes had been building up for months. "The teachers were drilling
it into our heads that we had to do our best work our junior year
if we wanted to get into the college of our choice. The stress of it
all totally overwhelmed me."

Ah, stress. We parents know a thing or two about that, don't
we? Our taxes are going up, our dollar value is on its way down,
and the boss is throwing deadlines at us like fastballs. If we don't
take on more clients, more accounts, more assignments, we'll
lose that lucrative promotion. And as if work weren't bad enough,
we've got to contend with mountains of bills, the joys of parent-
hood, and lawns that simply wilt in comparison with the Jones'
down the street. If only we could be kids again. Life was so much
easier then!

As stressed as they might feel themselves, parents of gifted
teens need to learn to recognize the types of pressures their kids
might be feeling. Don't assure yourself that because your teen is
so smart he'll have special insight into how to handle pressure—
in fact, some common characteristics of gifted students can exac-
erbate the challenges that nearly all teens face, including peer
relationships, college admissions, and the desire to succeed. If
you realize that your teen is likely to feel stressed and you know
the symptoms of excessive pressure, you'll know when and how
to step in if your teen needs you.

Why does my teen have trouble making close friends?

Lucy Hayes has watched a number of high-achieving teens
try to fit in during her more than twenty years teaching ninth-
grade gifted English in a public school. "When I watch the truly
gifted children go through high school, it definitely seems that the
biggest adjustment they have is their social adjustment. Much of
the time, they're younger than their peers and don't yet have the
social graces to completely fit in," she says. Sometimes, kids who

have been accelerated literally don't fit their environment, she points out. "One young man I taught was just too small to fit in the desk—he wanted to sit on top of the desk or on the floor because he was absolutely dwarfed by the furniture." He was very self-conscious about his size, Hayes says, but much happier to be with his intellectual, though not physical, peers.

Gifted kids and experts agree: The pressure of trying to fit in with the other kids often outweighs the demands of even the most difficult schoolwork. As they go through early adolescence (ages 11-15), most kids gradually detach themselves from their parents and other adults and re-define themselves according to the standards set up by their peer group. That's when "peer pressure" exerts itself most strongly. Linda Brody, director of the Study of Exceptional Talent at the Center for Talented Youth at the Johns Hopkins University, emphasizes that peer pressure to conform, which most adolescents feel, is not the same as pressure to feel socially accepted, which most gifted adolescents feel. "Because intellectual gaps and differences in interests often distance a gifted teen from his peers, achieving a satisfactory social situation becomes much more difficult," Brody explains. Witness the testimony of one highly gifted eighth-grade girl: "When your only true talent is your report card, you find it more difficult to prove yourself to the world. The major challenge in school for me is not the work, but fitting in."

James Webb, a professor and assistant dean at Wright State University and founding director of Supporting Emotional Needs of Gifted (SENG), blames gifted teens' problems with peer acceptance on American society's ambivalent attitude toward giftedness and high achievement. "On the one hand," he says, "leaders in our society say, 'We need our brightest minds; they're our nation's greatest resource.' But when you look for widespread support for high ability kids, it's simply not there." In its place is the myth that "a bright mind will find its own way." Gifted kids often get caught up in a stressful dilemma: Should I work up to my abilities and desires, exceed the norm, and be labeled a nonconformist? Or should I hold myself back to the norm and then have to deal with feeling bored, frustrated, and dishonest with myself? Webb insists that we need to understand pressures on gifted kids with this prevailing ambivalent attitude in mind.

On the other end of the spectrum is the myth that gifted people, in general, have problems. For instance, *Fortune* magazine characterized Microsoft founder Bill Gates as the world's "richest nerd," as though superior intellect automatically makes a person a wirehead. The idea is that Bill Gates, as a nerd, couldn't have business savvy or any such quality but, of course, he does. And even though such characterizations may be lighthearted in nature, the damage is done by the propagation of the myth, and gifted students have yet another challenge to face when it comes to social acceptance.

Brody and Webb agree that fitting in becomes still more challenging for gifted girls and for members of minority ethnic or religious groups. Gifted girls are more likely than gifted boys to conceal their intellectual abilities in the classroom and in social settings. "I have my friends from honors classes and friends from regular classes," writes one ninth-grade girl. "Sometimes I have to really be careful about what I say or talk about so as not to make the regular kids feel inferior. Since most of my time is spent in school, it's hard." Imagine the pressure of constantly having to censor what comes naturally to you, all for the sake of social acceptance! Although such self-censorship helps girls resemble the norm, odds are that the intellectual stifling will leave them extremely frustrated, Brody says.

Lucy Hayes has observed similar situations among gifted African-American students, especially the high-achieving boys. "Most of them really would love to be a role model for their peers, but their peers won't let them—they think it's really uncool to be that smart. When these boys are in the library working on a project and enjoying it, their friends come in and say, 'Come on, what's the matter with you?' And these kids are constantly being torn between loving to learn and being an outcast with their peers." Charles Richmond, a highly gifted sophomore and an African-American, says he experienced some problems with peers and faculty alike: "Sometimes, especially during my middle school years, teachers would just lump me in with all the black kids because that was the kind of student they got so often there. Then, when they began to see my intelligence, they had a hard time seeing past the initial stereotype that they had put me in." Charles also points out that, at times, being in a double minority can be "really very good because it gives me a chance to stand out positively at my school. The other kids see me as someone who can help them out by making the teachers see their abilities and not their race."

Besides social adjustment, what pressure is my teen facing?

Social adjustment might be a high-achieving teen's biggest problem, but it likely isn't his only problem. Chances are he's looking ahead to college applications and feeling a bit worried about that, too.

Most college-bound students worry about how their qualifications are adding up in comparison with the other students'. Will my aptitude test scores be high enough? Should I have more extracurricular activities? Gifted students (especially, for some reason, the more verbally talented and super-organized ones) tend to take these common concerns to the extreme. Lucy Hayes has seen plenty of her ninth-grade gifted students go on to sign up for four or five Advanced Placement courses their senior year. That may not be a good idea. "They don't realize that these courses are taught on the college level, and even in college you don't take a course every day of the week!" She adds that, each year, about ten percent of the kids in her gifted group insist, quite seriously, that their lives will end if they don't get into Harvard.

Often, gifted students will analyze and re-analyze the way their accomplishments and activities are going to look on the few sheets of paper read by a stranger in the college admissions office. Kelly

Cox, a gifted boy in the senior class at a very challenging private school in Atlanta, says, "Once I got my SAT scores back and saw how well I had done, I was worried that colleges would wonder why my grades didn't match up to all this aptitude I supposedly had. I was afraid that they would look at the disparity as a lack of effort, when actually I had very difficult coursework and demanding teachers." Charles Richmond, only a sophomore, has similar concerns: "I think about college a lot. It worries me, really, because I have a lot of interests outside of school. For example, a friend and I are developing a computer game—we're working on getting a grant to start a small company. I especially get concerned about my grades not reflecting the other things I do, such as my creativity and the way I think. As far as my capabilities being shown by my grades, that frightens me a lot."

Both boys have gripes about extracurricular activities and the emphasis that many parents place on them. "I'm on the school newspaper staff because it's something I enjoy, but I feel constant pressures to get involved in something else after school," says Richmond. "But given all the other things I'm working on—keeping my grades up and the projects I have outside of school—I just don't have the time for it." Cox finds it frustrating that certain activities "count" while others don't, or that the same activity counts in one context but not in another. "I consider myself musically gifted. I taught myself to play guitar and I practice at least a couple of hours a day, but my school doesn't care about that," he says. "Also, if you play varsity basketball, that's great, but if you come home from school every day and play basketball with your friends for hours, that doesn't count as an extracurricular activity. I don't understand."

Sometimes, pressure from parents—real or perceived—will magnify a gifted teen's worries. To begin with, the "gifted" label itself is a pressure, says Lucy Hayes. "Unfortunately, I work with a great many parents who think of giftedness as a social status symbol. I've had a lot of kids come to me in tears because of pressure from parents to live up to the label. I've seen gifted kids who cheat for all they're worth because their parents will kill them if they don't make an A." Psychologists warn parents against mistaking their own feelings and aspirations for their teens'. In other words, don't live your dreams vicariously through your teen.

Why does my teen push herself so hard, even if I don't?

Ironically, some of gifted kids' strengths—their intensity, sensitivity, attention to detail, and their powers of imagination and introspection—can also be their greatest weaknesses.

According to James Webb, mental and emotional intensity are practically universal among gifted students and are responsible for much of the emotional stress they feel. "There are some very predictable crises that occur," he says, "most commonly including power struggles with parents or teachers. The intensity combined with the ability to see how things might be prompts a child to question or challenge traditions, to take nothing on faith, and that makes other people uncomfortable."

This intensity also sets the stage for perfectionism, although experts disagree about its root cause. Webb contends that the ability to imagine how she might perform, coupled with emotional intensity, leads a student to have unduly high expectations of herself. Similarly, Linda Silverman of the Gifted Child Development Center in Denver relates perfectionism to exceptional abstract reasoning abilities: The gifted student can picture impressive accomplishments and faultless performances, but since his mental, motor, or social skills often can't make that picture into a reality, he feels extreme frustration. Linda Brody suggests that perfectionism comes from never having been sufficiently challenged. "Kids go through school programs that are too easy and they get accustomed to everything being easy and always getting the right answer. As a result, they can't handle being less than perfect in anything they do."

Whatever its exact cause, perfectionism can wear down a teen's self-esteem, leading to relentless self-criticism and a loss of self-worth. Some students will procrastinate in an attempt to avoid the agony of producing less-than-perfect work; others will stop producing altogether, feeling helpless. Webb finds that between fifteen and twenty percent of highly able children are significantly handicapped by perfectionism at some point during their academic careers. In a few cases, perfectionism will lead a teen to depression. Beware, parents: Healthy levels of perfectionism can simply lead to high-quality work, but if your teen's drive for success is leading him to trouble, you might need to alert a school counselor or a professional.

How do I know if my teen is feeling too much pressure, and what do I do then?

The symptoms might appear at school or at home. Lucy Hayes has noticed some not-so-subtle signs of excessive stress among her ninth-graders. "I've seen boxes of caffeine pills—and these are fourteen-year-olds! The other day, a girl said to me, 'You know, until this year, I never knew what coffee tasted like, and last night my mom had to make me two pots. I never fell asleep.'" She's seen students fall asleep involuntarily during class. She's seen kids who are home sick for days on end because "once they do get sick and have to stop pushing themselves for a moment, it all goes and they have to completely shut down."

Linda Brody names more symptoms: withdrawal, sleeplessness or oversleeping, frequent headaches, dropping grades, difficulties in relationships with friends and family members, and being generally grumpy. "All of these are possible symptoms of some kind of distress, and if it's a child who is under heavy social or academic pressure, that's certainly something that should be examined," she says.

There's a lot you can do to help your teen with pressure, and it's never too late to start. First, make yourself available to your teen—listen well, don't interrupt, and try to give advice only when he or she asks for it. Grant your teen space and privacy. Try to model achievement in a wide range of interests without perfectionism. Encourage self-management and resilience in your teen—you might have to provide a reminder that he or she is in a minority and doesn't have to believe in the opinions of an uninformed majority. Set aside time to spend exclusively with your teen, but don't try to be a buddy; instead, remain in the role of parent. And make it clear to your teen through your words and your body language that you love and value your teen for himself and not for his accomplishments.

Linda Brody grants that parenting gifted children is an enormous task. She encourages parents to strive for what the Center for Talented Youth calls the "optimal match," a balance between a child's interests and abilities and his educational programming, both academic and social. "Each child needs a unique match; experiment until you find the match that makes your child happy and successful."

No single solution fits every case. Charles Richmond describes how his mother, a single parent, helps him deal with stress: "After sixteen years with me, my mom understands how I work. When she sees that I'm getting too stressed out, she'll stop me. So while I may be getting a lot of flak from the teachers, like, 'Oh, Charles, I've seen your brain, you're so brilliant, you can do better than this,' my mom says, 'We know it's there. We've seen you put it on paper before. We know you've got it, so just do the best you can for right now.' And I really appreciate that, because as long as I get that support from her, and as long as she knows I'm doing my best, she'll fight for me. I know she's on my side."

While Charles counts on help from his mother, Amy Martin needed more control over her own schedule. After Amy was finished letting off steam, she and her parents sat down together and talked the situation out. They identified the several activities that meant the most to Amy and agreed to let her manage her schedule by herself. "So far it's working out fine," Amy reports. "I'm glad I let them know how I was feeling, and I'm really glad they laid off and let me be in charge of my life. They allowed me to take full control when I felt completely out of control, and that was the solution for me."

The Brains to Be Happy

Passing life's many multiple choice tests may be the toughest challenge of all— and the only one that really matters.

The following discussion took place in Durham, North Carolina. Participating in the discussion were Lea Davis, David Hartman and Michael Yoo, all in their early twenties and all identified earlier in life as academically talented.

Lea Davis has a bachelor of arts degree from Duke University. She is currently waiting tables as she seeks her career path.

David Hartman has a bachelor of arts degree from the University of North Carolina at Chapel Hill. He is the production manager of a publishing firm.

Michael Yoo has a bachelor of science degree from Harvard University. He is a PhD student in physics at MIT.

Where has college taken you?

Michael: I have chosen to pursue an academic career, specifically physics. I ultimately envision myself as a university professor teaching and doing research in physics. I learned about pursuing physics or a scientific career largely from my parents. Both my parents are research chemists, so science was always an important part of our household. But I didn't make my decision to pursue physics in particular probably until college, when I had a number of good professors and good experiences in physics courses.

My high school education was very broad, but I knew that I had talents in math and science. My college education was quite focused. I took a lot of physics classes and a lot of math classes. However, I took a lot of courses outside the sciences in college, partly because of the requirements and also—more importantly—because I was interested.

David: I focused more on work from an early age. I started working in graphic arts at age fourteen during the summers, and the thought of working always was more appealing than school. I think money was probably was a big part of that. I worked through the summer at fourteen and fifteen, got a car, started working during school and focused most of my energy on *that*. And school, I would say, suffered as a result. The rewards on the other side have been pretty good because now I have a good job and own part of a company.

Lea: My career has not started. I'm waiting tables, and I don't want a career in it, although it's paying the bills right now. I've never been really focused. I've studied what I was interested in, and I went through college taking whatever I was interested in. I loved it. I had a wonderful experience, I learned a whole lot, I feel very enriched, but I wasn't working toward a career. I can envision myself doing several different things right now. Sometimes

I think about staying in academics, but I haven't been serious enough about it yet to start a PhD program.

I don't reflect on it that often, but I never had any epiphany or any moment when I knew things were special. I never had an angel come down and touch me. I guess I was always ahead of kids and knew it.

If the writing career I want doesn't flourish... Well, I feel like I can do a lot of things, but it's hard to convince someone who doesn't share my mindset that I really could. I've had jobs. I worked for a managing editor of a journal at Duke, and I took her place for six months while she had a baby. I *was* her for six months. I had three weeks to learn her job and did it. And I feel like I can do a lot of jobs and I've proven in the opportunities that I've had that I can do good work. If writing doesn't pan out, then I will choose something else.

I feel like the loser of the bunch. I'm not satisfied with what I'm doing now, but I don't think the future is a loss at all. I'll find my track very shortly.

What was your experience in middle school and high school?

David: I always felt as though I fit in. No one ever seemed to notice that I was smart. I never felt out of place. I tried to fit in. I never just sat there—if I *knew* the answer in class, I said it. I never muted my intelligence in any way or purposely made an effort to distinguish myself or to blend in.

I think I change easily from one situation to another. If I'm at the gas station and I need some help, I know how to talk to someone with a different background. I've always adapted, but I never felt like I was ostracized or set apart because of intelligence, though I knew people who were. I saw that happen to other people.

Michael: My experience was quite different. Throughout junior high and high school I was apart—I was actually quite sepa-

rate—from my peers. I was noticeably different because I took classes with students who were two, three, four, sometimes even five
years ahead of me. I was very fortunate in that I had a number
of friends who were very close to my own age. So I never felt
ostracized, but certainly I felt different. The situation I was in made
it difficult not to feel different.

For example, in eighth grade, throughout the day I took
classes with eighth graders, ninth graders, tenth graders, eleventh
graders, and twelfth graders. So, depending on the time of the day,
I was with a different crowd. The reason I say I was very fortunate especially not to feel ostracized is that, among the classes I
took with the older students, I developed friendships. I felt like
a kid brother in a lot of those classes—apart from just the day-
to-day interaction with those students in classes. I guess I felt
different but never ostracized.

I don't know that I'm necessarily the typical case. I was very
fortunate that the students I was with were very accepting. And
I've been fortunate to be reasonably outgoing. I've always made
friends easily, so that made things easier. I've seen other gifted students—not so much in school, but in other situations—have a
more difficult time relating to older students, perhaps because
they are more introverted, perhaps because the students who are
around them feel threatened by younger, more talented students.

It's hard for me to speak about what I think is typical because
the local school district in which my parents live was, I think,
quite progressive. A number of students at any given time were
taking advanced courses, and so the atmosphere among the
administrators was very much one of bending over backwards to
help the students.

Lea: I went through middle school in a local school district. Then
for high school I moved to a private school and the reason for that
pretty much had to do with academics. I had a more difficult
time than Michael did, for sure. There were a lot of really very
bright kids in the small town where I'm from, but the school dis-

trict was very traditional. They wouldn't allow any room for advancing someone or for compromise. They were into making everyone fit the norm. If you were in this group, then you were reading that book—and you were nowhere else. I can remember reading the same books from one year to the next. It was a big fight to get any little extra thing. My parents were supportive, my mom especially. She founded the parents of gifted kids group and she always tried to push for me.

Things started getting bad after I went to TIP. A lot of us took the SAT in seventh grade, and I think I was the only child that year to qualify to go to the programs at Duke. And I went, I loved it, and then I came back home. And school was just horrible after that because I felt like I had been free for awhile and then put back in this really stifling curriculum.

We had a really, really bright English class. My mom took the suggested reading list for the TIP kids to the teacher, and she said, "Lea was at this program this summer and this is some of the stuff she used, and I thought it would be a good idea for you to have." The teacher just went wild. She said, "They're in eighth grade. They don't need to be reading high school books." My mom said, "But these are really gifted kids, they've been reading on a high school level, and these are the books they should have read." So that teacher hated me. I'm not just saying this with animosity. The teachers felt like I was different, like my mom was pushy.

What kind of pressures do teens feel?

Lea: I switched to a private school in the ninth grade, and things were still difficult. I played a lot of sports. I did a lot of activities. I remember I tried out for cheerleading at the end of ninth grade and made it. I was really athletic. I made it because I was good. And this group of popular boys cornered me on campus after the team was announced, and they said, "Did you have to put your GPA on your cheerleader application?" I said, "Yeah, everybody did." And they said, "Well, that explains it." Here I switched schools and I'm so much happier and this happens. But it wasn't all bad. I had some really good experiences, too. But those are some examples of what can happen.

David: I think that one reason I *didn't* feel separated was that in my case a lot of students qualified for TIP. I don't know how many participated, but a lot qualified from the school where I was enrolled, so a lot of people were on that level. And there were thirty of us who were taking math that was "two years ahead" of everybody else. I wasn't sitting there in a class with people four or five years older than me. I was in a school system that was progressive. There were a lot of people in that same gifted and talented group, and we moved along together. So I think that made a big difference in not feeling like we were different.

Michael: For me, the middle school years were pretty difficult. I think they are a difficult time for any child regardless of whether you are identified as academically talented or not. Most of my friends were grade school friends with whom I had been taking classes, had been playing with—neighborhood kids—and we all ended up going to the same junior high. So we continued our friendships there. High school, like I said before, was like a bit of a jumble initially. I had older friends and friends my age. Most of the friendships I developed in high school came through activities outside the classroom.

I think—going back to the junior high school years—one of the tough things about being identified as academically talented as a young teenager is that there is definitely a sense of pressure to fit in with the crowd. But that pressure tends to diminish as you get older and become more sure of yourself. And anything that tends to identify you as being something different can be an added pressure, especially at an age when you are very sensitive to that kind of thing.

David: Sometimes if you are in a situation where you see a lot of people really trying to fit in, you think, "Gosh, that's kind of silly." Yet you really have this strong urge to be part of the group. I suppose this is the same for all kids. I'm not sure how much difference there really is between anyone of us and anybody else I went to school with. Maybe we thought a little bit more about those things: "Hey, that pair of Air Jordans doesn't do anything better for my feet than this pair of Keds." Yet you still had an urge to fit in. You questioned it more, and that made it even harder sometimes when you were trying to fit in. You realized that you didn't want to care—but you *did* care, because the pressure was so great to do this or that.

What's it like for teens when they finish school?

Lea: It's really reassuring to go out in the world and be in situations and succeed in situations where no one knows you. When I really sit back and think about it, I think that is one reason why I'm only doing what I am doing right now. I was very little other than "academic" through twenty years of school, a lot of summers, and a lot of summer programs. All my achievements in track and cross-country didn't seem to count. I think I really needed a year or two by myself to find out what I was besides "academic" and what else I can do. I wondered at first if I was just a loser, since I don't have a job yet. And then I realized that I have really gained a lot of confidence in myself. I am much more independent. I needed a year or two to find out who I was outside of school.

David: There is one fear I have faced in coming out of school with a liberal arts degree—that there wasn't any career that was set professionally. I've got a number of close friends, and they are ending up with professional degrees. I felt some fear walking out into the world, but I have what I have and that's great. Sometimes I feel like there is no fall-back position, but I'm sure that I would make it if something happened.

Michael: I think that once you get out into the real world, say, after college, you quickly realize that to succeed in life and— more importantly—to be happy, there are more things than just academic or career skills that really play a role in your happiness and the way you feel about yourself. Now, even being in an academic career where academics are valid, I think being academically talented or being identified as such doesn't help much when you are trying to make a career decision. By the time you are in the working world and are competing with other people for a position, whether you are a year younger or a year older doesn't matter anymore. What really matters is what kind of skills you have, how you relate with people, whether people will enjoy working with you. And, from your own point of view, it matters whether you enjoy what you do. I think all of those issues aren't really affected one way or another by how advanced you might have been at age twelve.

How do talented teens pick up life skills to make decisions?

Lea: You learn it.

David: Not in school.

Michael: You learn it by doing it.

David: I learned as much in college outside of the classroom as I did in. I lived a rather sheltered precollege existence. I think that a lot of the things I learned in college were social. You deal with more people. In high school, you get up, you go to school, you go home, and you live your life. But college is more of a complete environment, and I learned a lot from that environment that was as important as what I learned in the classroom.

What advice would teens give their parents?

Lea: Let us do things for ourselves, no matter how hard it is to let us go. Stay at a bit of a distance, no matter how much we seem to suffer. Be supportive. Be there to do things that only parents can do. But don't act for us.

Michael: I don't know if there is advice I would give my parents. Looking back I am very happy with my childhood and the opportunities I was given both in school and out of school by my parents. What my parents gave me most of all was a fairly strong sense of self-esteem. Regardless of how I did or what I did, my parents always made it clear that they were supportive and behind me and that they were proud of who I was. That was an important thing. I think the adolescent years are a time when children in general tend to be very self doubting, and I know many people find those years to be very painful. My parents really instilled in me a sense of pride in who I was. That, I think, is the greatest gift they gave me, apart from everything they've done for me in school and outside of school.

What about success and happiness?

Michael: Five years from now I see myself trying to be a tenured professor in physics in some university in the United States. Ten years from then I hope I've gotten that tenure and will be teaching and doing research.

But as far as when I'll feel successful, I really have to mark that as when I'm going to actually grow up. It always seems that grown ups know what they want to do. You knew when you got to a certain age you'd figure out what life had in store for you. Now that I seem to be at that age, I still don't know what's in store for me.

A lot of what it means to be successful, I translate as what it means to be happy. I think there are a lot of things in life besides work. There's a spouse, there's children. And, I think, knowing how to have the right balance between those is when I finally say I am successful.

David: A wonderful façade that parents put up for their children is that they know what they are doing, that they are where they want to be. But I'm not sure. If you looked at your parents when you were a kid, you thought, "Yeah, they know what they want to do." I think most people our age would be surprised at how normal the way we are feeling right now is. I think that probably goes on throughout life.

Where will I be in five, ten, fifteen years? I have no idea, and I don't want to know. I think I'm happy doing what I'm doing now and I can see it evolving into a lot of other things. How will I know when I'm successful? I feel successful now.

Lea: I have some scenarios I think about. I think about starting a private school. I think about sitting at a desk with a pile of manuscripts and picking them up and seeing if they go on and how they go on—being an editor. Both of those would make me really happy, as would some other things. But I don't know yet what I'll be doing in five or ten years. I think that I will be happy, and I'm not that worried about it. I feel like I have grown up in the past year or so, because I realize that I'm OK no matter what I'm doing. I am successful. I am independent. I am smart. I'm a person *outside* of being smart, too. I have a lot of options and I have the power to consider them and take the ones I want and pass on the ones I don't. The future is open and I like it that way.

Right now I'm happy with myself, but I'm not happy with what I'm doing. I've got personal success and not career success. I'll be happy when I have both.

Index